STEALING HOME

A Coach's Quest to Maximize Run Production in High School Baseball

KENNY HUGO
AND
JOHN ALEXANDER

with a Foreword by
Paul Mainieri, Head Baseball Coach
Louisiana State University

Copyright © 2014 Kenny Hugo
All rights reserved.

ISBN: 1495385698
ISBN 13: 9781495385698

What baseball coaches are saying about *Stealing Home*:

Kenny Hugo has written an unusual and compelling book, one that I recommend to all coaches, players, and fans. Manufacturing runs is a big part of the college game now, as well as the high school game, especially with today's less potent bats. Many of Kenny's philosophies and ideas are currently embraced by coaches and players on collegiate diamonds across the country.

Kenny worked our select baseball camp several summers in a row. Like our other camp coaches, he was assigned a team to coach, in addition to his instructional duties. The first time I watched one of his teams play, they scored a baserunner from second on a ground ball to the infield. By week's end, Kenny's players were sprinting to first on a walk, running the bases aggressively and intelligently, and constantly pressuring whatever defense his team was facing that day.

Stealing Home also provides excellent practice drills for coaches and players that will enhance habits that generate run production. If I were starting my coaching or playing career today, this is a book I'd want to read.

One of Kenny's better high school players, a young man who was highly recruited as a junior, became seriously ill in his senior year. Everyone backed off of the kid. Kenny made a trip down to Tallahassee to talk with us personally about the young man and explained that he would recover, and that he was going to make someone a fine collegian. Kenny's player not only became part of our starting lineup, he led us in hitting in the College World Series.

Mike Martin, Head
Baseball Coach
Florida State University

⚾ ⚾ ⚾

Kenny's book is a MUST read for all men and women who claim to be or want to be called "Coach." Lessons from someone as knowledgeable as Kenny can possibly get you through some difficult times not only on the diamond but in life as well.

> Randy Putman, Head Coach, Wallace St. Hanceville (Alabama) NJCAA Hall of Fame Member with 900 career wins and six World Series appearances on the NJCAA Division 1 level

Stealing Home is a must read for all baseball coaches and fans of the game. This book applies real life stories of high school baseball and explains favorite drills and teaching points at the same time. The stories of the coaching career (of Kenny Hugo) are enough to keep any fan reading, but getting to hear the coaching points and execution of the running game from a coach's standpoint makes you feel like you are right there in the dugout. For any high school coach looking for an advantage in the running game—this is your way to get to the next base.

Danny Wallace, Head Coach
Flower Mound High School
2014 Texas 5-A State Champions

FOREWORD

I have been blessed to coach this great game for many years. I have been even more blessed to benefit from outstanding mentorship, from my dad, Demie, coaches I had throughout my playing career, and my colleagues—coaches in other programs. I believe that much of my success has been taking advantage of what I learned along the way from smart baseball people.

I have also been blessed with outstanding young players at every stop along my college coaching career. In fact, these have been marvelous young men, who were capable of gaining admission to some of the finest schools in the nation: St. Thomas University in Miami (FL), the United States Air Force Academy, the University of Notre Dame, and Louisiana State University. And, not only were they solid citizens and good students, they were exceptionally talented ballplayers who were able to make the rosters made up of other very talented players. Regarding their baseball talents, I believe that every one of them possessed some God-given, inherent talent that cannot be taught or coached. But, even more than that, most of these players were taught well about how to play the game. For that, I give their high school and youth coaches a great deal of credit. I simply would not be able to find these kinds of players—enabling our school to compete for a national championship every year—without the superb instruction and leadership they received before coming to college.

So, I am pleased and grateful for Kenny and John for contributing to the greater knowledge of the game, for their dedication to many high school and youth coaches who are working hard to be good teachers and motivational leaders. This is a fascinating and compelling book—a solid piece of work that everyone, including college coaches, high school coaches, and young players will be able to use in improving their knowledge and skills.

This book, the only one I know of that is written specifically for coaching offensive baseball at the high school level, captures much of the knowledge that is indispensable for coaches of amateur baseball up through high school, and even into college. The game of baseball is far more intricate than the casual observer might notice. Even with high school players, there is a lot going on in games and, indeed, during all the preparation for the season and each game. For that reason, it is great to see someone record for the rest of us some of the finer points of coaching the game, of using strategy as well as physical talent, of teaching the right skills and attitudes, and handling the tough decisions in offensive game situations.

Kenny Hugo is a great story teller! His methods for constructing a potent offensive lineup is a must-read. When you consider offensive strategy, as this book does, it's all about maximizing run production, any way you can. At the college level, the need to utilize creative offensive strategies is growing annually. Bats are less lively, and we are facing outstanding pitching and solid defenses every time we take the field. Much of Kenny's offensive philosophy applies to the college game as it's played today.

For young players, there is a wealth of information and a great series of drills on building your individual offensive skills. And, for coaches, there is solid instruction on how to build a program, and how to relate to young baseball players. If you plan to coach and want to build a first-class program, put this book on your reading list.

Paul Mainieri, Head Baseball Coach Louisiana State University

This book is dedicated to

... Robert Wayne behind the plate, to Bob K. and Albie up the middle, and to Horace and Jerome at the corners, an infield for a lifetime of seasons ....

... And, to Dan Romero, John Zinda, Bill Arce, and all coaches of youth and amateur athletes who teach, inspire, and give far more than they receive.

"Or we can blaze. Become legends in our own time, strike fear in the heart of mediocre talent everywhere! We can scald dogs, put records out of reach! Make the stands gasp. They'll speak our names in hushed tones, 'those guys are animals' they'll say! We can lay it on the line, bust a gut, show them a clean pair of heels. We can sprint the turn on a spring breeze and feel the winter leave our feet! We can, by God, let our demons loose and just wail on!"

From *Once a Runner* by John L. Parker, Jr.

PREFACE

"It is not the critic who counts; not the man who points out how the strong man stumbles, or where the doer of deeds could have done them better. The credit belongs to the man who is actually in the arena, whose face is marred by dust and sweat and blood; who strives valiantly; who errs, who comes short again and again, because there is no effort without error and shortcoming; but who does actually strive to do the deeds; who knows great enthusiasms, the great devotions; who spends himself in a worthy cause; who at the best knows in the end the triumph of high achievement, and who at the worst, if he fails, at least fails while daring greatly, so that his place shall never be with those cold and timid souls who neither know victory nor defeat."

Excerpt from the speech by President Theodore Roosevelt entitled, *Citizenship In A Republic* delivered at the Sorbonne, in Paris, France on April 23, 1910

In baseball, coaches are "in the arena." In fact, more so than any other sport, baseball managers and coaches are part of the game. They are on the field of play. They wear a baseball uniform. They are integral to the game, clearly visible to the other participants and spectators. Their decisions are mostly obvious and the results quickly apparent. They are scrutinized and criticized, sometimes lauded, but never discounted.

This book is about coaching the greatest game in the world—baseball—at the high school level. And, it is focused on the offensive aspects of baseball at that level. The idea is to capture some of the thoughts and considerations for coaching at this level, based on our experience in that arena.

I first met Kenny Hugo when we were both forty years and some change past our high school playing careers. Our meeting had nothing to do with baseball, and we are both now pursuing careers completely unrelated to the sport. For some reason during the course of our session together, I mentioned that I had just finished writing a book on pitching. Which I had. And Kenny said, "Well, I used to coach high school baseball, and I'd love to read it."

Our friendship, and our shared passion for baseball, grew from there. Very quickly it became apparent that Kenny, though he was long retired from coaching, still had some stories to tell. So I said "Why don't you write a book on coaching high school baseball?" Well, the idea rattled around in his noggin for a couple of weeks, and finally he said, "I'll do it." He was also quick to say, "I don't know if anybody will be interested in reading it, but I'll tell the story of my coaching career and you can do what you want with it."

Now, understand, it's not the first baseball rodeo for Kenny or me. I grew up on baseball in California. I was fortunate to live in a neighborhood in California where a fine gentleman and superb baseball man lived, who was about my parents' age and had a son about my age. Dan Romero organized our neighborhood kids into what was a 1960s version of a modern travel team—a local team on which I played for roughly eight years until I went to high school.

Dan was a superb teacher of the game, and a remarkable fundraiser. He was a Hispanic gentleman who worked in what was known as the produce markets in Los Angeles. He went to work at the markets early each morning, and in the afternoon picked us up from school in his nine-passenger station wagon. He then drove us home to change, picked us up again, drove us to the park to practice (all year, by the way; most days of the week), and then brought us home. He had been a pitcher, so when I showed some aptitude for it, he taught me to pitch. Until then, I was a catcher. Because of him, I never played Little League. We started out as the Whitehurst Beavers (because Dan lived on Whitehurst Drive). He arranged games all over the LA area. Then, we became the Los Angeles Produce Merchants (our sponsors). And, he got us into what was known as the "Golden State League," an exceptionally well run amateur baseball organization which had various age divisions all the way up to teens. Even when little, we played major league rules (metal spikes, leading off, stealing, etc.) though on a smaller field. What a great start!

Dan also was a fine golfer who taught me that game as well (not just the swing, but the etiquette—with lessons on the course, never charging us a dime). He taught all of us sports, but also how to be athletes and gentlemen. What he did for me was to instill the love of the game of baseball. I lived and died with the Walter Alston Dodgers (you may have heard of Sandy Koufax and Don Drysdale). That youth baseball experience springboarded me into high school ball, where I fell in love with working on the bump in the middle of the infield. I later pitched in college before heading off to more serious endeavors. As family man, I coached my son and his travel team and stayed connected to the game as best I could. But I never got it out of my blood. You have to love baseball to write an entire book on pitching.

I still follow the game closely, but I never coached organized high school baseball, except for summer ball. And to hear Kenny tell it firsthand was a little like being allowed to crawl inside the third base coach's head at the ballpark. I mean, I knew the coach knew how many outs there were and who was on deck, but I was fascinated to hear all the things that were going through his head in that little rectangular box of chalk over there beyond third base.

Kenny grew up in the South, but he started his coaching career in California. And he coached some stellar high school clubs. He doesn't talk much about records and wins and losses, but I know for a fact that at one point one of his teams in Georgia won 30 straight games and was ranked no. 1 in that state's largest classification of schools. At another time he had a ball club that was 39-2 over a 41 game span in two seasons. That's pretty good in any league. He's sent players to the pros and a slew of them to major colleges. Kenny coached in four states, sometimes building programs from scratch, and his recollections are fascinating. I heard a lot of them as we ate barbeque and discussed ideas for the book in a local restaurant, and it quickly became apparent that he had a lot of baseball to get out of his system. For him, I think this book served as a way to close the door on a long and important chapter in his life. Several times during our meetings he would recall a story for me, then follow it up by saying, "I had forgotten that happened."

For me, our meetings reconnected me to the game, and in a way that I had never considered before. I had always seen the game through a pitcher's eyes. You know: What's the count, where am I in the lineup, what did this guy hit last time up, what's my best pitch today, things like that. And when it was time to swing the bat and run the bases I did that as I was coached. But to break the game down to its roots, and to practice and implement fundamental movements that result in a kid's ability to, say, bunt for a base hit, or execute the delayed steal, these are things I had never considered from a coach's point of view. I also never thought a lot about what goes on in a coach's mind when there are runners aboard in a live game situation. Believe me, if all high school coach are like Kenny, the wheels are turning.

This book is a former high school coach explaining how to maximize run production. And Kenny provides his favorite hitting and baserunning drills and practice ideas. But it's much more than that. It's storytelling. It's Kenny recalling baserunning mistakes and arguments with umpires and failed coaching moves and all the other things that go into a coach learning how to practice his craft. He'll tell you in this book: Everything he learned about coaching high school baseball, he learned from making mistakes. In my former career, I flew high-performance jet fighter aircraft. And the first thing we pilots would do after every flight was get together and break down everything that happened. And go over it step by step. And then figure out how to avoid mistakes in the future, how not to repeat a failed effort. Well, that's what coaching is about. At least it was for Kenny.

You'll be amazed at how many misunderstandings and instances of failed communication Kenny will recall. One in particular makes me laugh out loud every time I think about it. It involves a kid getting but misinterpreting the "take" sign. But I'll leave it for you to read, and I hope you enjoy these misadventures as much as I did.

Kenny also recalls stories of contests where things went just right, just according to plan, and those are wonderful passages as well. Either way, he's telling you what he went through and what he was thinking while things were happening on and off the field . . . .

We both were fortunate in baseball and in life, but our stories are not really that unique. As the result of our mentors and early starts in the game, our love of baseball spans all the facets of the game. We understand, as savvy baseball fans do, that baseball is a deceptively complex game. It is played on many levels simultaneously. Baseball people know there are lots of strategic mind games going on while the physical aspects of the game and the season take place—different levels of activity unfolding simultaneously during an at bat, an inning, a game, a series, a season. The mechanics of the game are important, as in any sport. But, real fans of the game are into all the mental games within the game—pitching strategy, approaches to each at bat, defensive positioning, defensive plays, offensive plays, baserunning, manipulating the lineup, setting up pitching for the late innings, and thinking about the next game.

As we think about playing the game, and then coaching the game, we think first about individual matchups (pitchers versus hitters). But, then our thoughts as coaches turn to tactics (the various approaches employed on each pitch throughout the game), short-term and long-term considerations (the game we are in, the next game, the season), the ebb and flow of strategy (plays) based on previous encounters, and the mind games always unfolding between opposing coaches and between and among the players. This stuff is fun, and even more so as our knowledge and experience grow.

We recognize that coaching baseball requires a unique combination of objective statistical evidence and trends, yet a reliance on the subjective experience of players and coaches gained over time. The balance between these two represents the style of the coach. The choices we make as coaches, managing the game, reflect that style.

Baseball people know there are no perfect answers or solutions in baseball, either in mechanics or in strategy. Everyone has their idea of how to teach and coach the game of baseball. As in other sports, there is a flow to the game, but there are also very measureable and objective events, hence the extensive use of statistics. Decisions are very discrete and immediately executed, with measurable, and certainly obvious, outcomes. The outcome of coach's decisions are clear and obvious successes or failures. So, the coach is considered a hero or a goat—right away. Sometimes, it is all about playing the percentages; sometimes it is all about playing hunches; sometimes it is about taking calculated risks—gambling on a play or a player based on a feel for the game. Always, there is at some level a tradeoff in benefits (positive outcomes) and risks (potential failures) in the choices we make in managing the game. It does not always work out.

So, this book is really a collection of Kenny's coaching experiences at the high school level, that serve as great illustrations of the options and choices available to coaches in their approach to the game. Since there are no right answers written on stone tables, this book is not a manual for coaches. Rather, it is a collection of Kenny's wisdom over many years. We fully expect that others may disagree with some of the philosophies expressed here. But, that is the beauty of the game—since there are no right answers, the debate and the discussion are as important as the answers. We have found that we know a lot less about the game then we thought we did. We have learned over time that our knowledge increases with every discussion. And in that mindset, perhaps what Kenny wrote here will help both aspiring and experienced coaches think about the many facets of this complex game.

This volume is all about the offensive side of the game. There is plenty to talk about here related to the offensive aspects of baseball at the high school level. And, we believe that baseball at the high school level is somewhat unique. There are aspects of the game at this level that may not translate to lower and higher levels of ball due to the physical attributes of the players and the nature of baseball seasons at the various levels. But, then again, there are many kernels of wisdom here that may apply at every level.

The methodology we used here is illustrating key aspects of coaching the offensive side of high school baseball through Kenny's anecdotes and experiences. Again, there are no right and wrong ways to play and coach the game; there are some ideas that seem to work, most of the time but not always. As coaches, we strive to teach the game based on our understanding of the game and our experiences. We manage the game based on those same experiences. We make decisions, usually with little time to reflect, and based on a mental calculation of the risks and benefits, and hope that our hunches pay off—they don't always. But, as President Roosevelt stated so eloquently, it is the man (the coach) in the arena who must make the call and then enjoy the fruits of success or suffer the indignation of failure. And, then, press on to the next one.

The intent of this book is certainly to impart a bit of wisdom from Kenny's years of experience. But, it is also to encourage coaches to think about the many facets of the offensive game of baseball at the high school level, and to make their own minds up about what to consider and how to execute. If it helps coaches to do that, we will have achieved our purpose.

John Alexander

John Alexander, my trusty co-author and good friend, encouraged me to write this book. Without that, I wouldn't have done it. John, a former college pitcher, had just finished writing a book on pitching. Reading his book and talking about it with him springboarded us both into the project that became *Stealing Home*.

I coached high school baseball in four states for more years than I care to remember. What I do recall is how many mistakes I made, and how lost I was when I began running practices, making out lineup cards, and standing in the third base coaching box. I read every instructional book I could get my hands on. A couple of books full of baseball drills, written by Danny Litwhiler and Jerry Kendall, were especially helpful. But as you will read in these pages, nothing prepares you for the unexpected challenges that arise in coaching.

How you develop the talent you've got, and more specifically, how you maximize run production on offense, is the subject of this book. It's fair to say, I think, that reading a book like this in my first year of coaching would have been extremely beneficial. Though like most coaches, I only truly learned through experience. You can tell a person that a stove is hot until you're blue in the face, and they may or may not process it. But until they accidentally burn their hand on the thing, you're never sure if the lesson is getting through. As Robert Penn Warren said, "Every truth is paid for with a little blood." In coaching parlance, every mistake you make produces an out, one you can't afford to give your opponents. So even if I had had this book available to me when I starting coaching, I'm not sure how much I would have absorbed. Experience is indeed the best teacher. But if you're smart enough to read about my mistakes, maybe you can avoid a few of your own.

Young baseball players are becoming stronger, faster, and more athletic. Pitchers throw harder. Balls are hit farther. But there are many ways to maximize your talents that can enhance your natural athletic ability.

So we hope these pages serve to inspire and instruct young players, too. There are lots of drills and ideas here that players can incorporate into their daily routines. If you play the game for a while, you'll play for a lot of different coaches. So the more you know about the game, the better off you'll be. Becoming your own best baseball friend, coaching yourself through slumps, and relying on a few trusted lessons to help you in hitting and base running is a good thing. We hope this book helps you maximize your offensive talent.

Enjoy. Laugh. Love the game. Play hard. Play fast.

Good luck.

Kenny Hugo

TABLE OF CONTENTS

Foreword vii
Preface xiii
List of Figures xxvii
Introduction 1
High School Baseball Coaching Commandments 11
Chapter One: Praying for Victory 15
Chapter Two: It Don't Come Easy 23
Chapter Three: To a Blind Mule, A Wink's as Good as a Nod 35
Chapter Four: Life is a Carnival 41
Chapter Five: You Can't Steal First 49
    One Run Better 50
    Touch Home More Often than the Opposition 52
    High School Offense 53
    Keeping Up a Scare 54
    Aggressiveness and Speed 56
    Aggressive Hitting 58
    A Few Basic Habits 60
    That's The Old Pepper 65
Chapter Six: Nobody Ever "Looked" One Out of the Park 69
    It's a Balancing Act 72
    Good Launch Position 74
    Get Your Chin On It 78
    The Weight Transfer 81
    Hitting Off a Firm Front Side 86
    Hitting the Breaking Ball 89
    Keep Your Own Counsel 92

Chapter Seven: Building a Good Lineup 95
   "Rabbits" 95
   Building a Good Lineup 98
   The Leadoff Hitter 98
   Forget The Sacrifice Bunt 101
   The 2-Spot 104
   The Hit and Run 105
   The Number 3 Hitter 106
   Middle of the Lineup 110
   "Big Dogs" 111
Chapter Eight: Offensive Signs and Signals 115
   Selecting An Indicator 115
   Signing Without an Indicator 121
   Non-Signal Hand Gestures and Yells 128
Chapter Nine: Bunting for a Base Hit 133
   Choosing Your Spot: The Long Throw from Third 137
   The Daily Bunting Game 143
   How To Bunt for a Hit 144
Chapter Ten: Coaching Baserunning 151
   Practice Like You Play 154
   Coaching Your Hitters (and Baserunners) 159
   Knowing the Rules 165
   Primary and Secondary Leads 167
   Combination Drill 170
   Walking It Up 173
   Utilizing the Stopwatch and Picking Your Spots 173
   The Ultimate Combo Baserunning-Team Defense Drill 177
   Adding Flavor to an Already Excellent Drill 180
Chapter Eleven: Stealing and Other Baserunning Plays 185
   Executing the Delayed Steal of Second 186
   The Straight Steal of Second 189
   Sliding 190
   Stealing Second Against a Lefty 193

    Leading Off Second. 195
    Straight Line and 2-Out Leads Off Second 195
    Stealing Third Base 196
    Leading Off Third 202
    Stealing Home 207
    First and Third Versus a Lefty Play. 220
    First and Second Jam Up Play 224
Chapter Twelve: Have it Your Way 229

LIST OF FIGURES

Figure 1. Hitting the ball where's it's pitched. 63
Figure 2. Playing pepper with a purpose. 65
Figure 3. Concentration at the point of contact. 80
Figure 4. Shifting the weight from back to front. 82
Figure 5. Review your signal package every day
during stretching exercises. 116
Figure 6. The "bunt for a base hit," and all bunts, work
best as a surprise weapon. 136
Figure 7. Communicating with multiple runners on the same play. . . 155
Figure 8. Hitters should check the third base coach on every pitch. . . 159
Figure 9. Beat it out or go for two. 162
Figure 10. Communication is the key to success. 163
Figure 11. Practice the art of baserunning and defense simultaneously. . 171
Figure 12. Make a line drive go through. 183
Figure 13. Executing the straight steal. 189
Figure 14. Straight line (0 out and 1 out) and 2-out leads from
second base. 197
Figure 15. Down in foul and back in fair. 203
Figure 16. Practicing the steal of home. 209
Figure 17. Runner in a rundown between third and home. 212

INTRODUCTION

"I loved the game," Shoeless Joe went on. "I'd have played for food money. I'd have played for free and worked for food. It was the game, the parks, the smells, the sounds."

Shoeless Joe Jackson Comes To Iowa by W. P. Kinsella

You start out thinking you're going to teach your slower-footed starters the fine points of the delayed steal, and end up counseling a kid whose Dad has cancer. My second year as a head coach in Texas, four of my players, three position players who were starters, and a pitcher in the starting rotation, all had family members suffering with serious cancer. Two Dads, a Mom, and a younger sister.

I don't know if I handled it right. Can't even really remember how I handled it, if at all. I know I didn't do much yelling that year. That's 4 kids out of 18 who wake up every day knowing that one of their family members is battling for their life and may not survive. I've attended more than my share of baseball coaching clinics, but counseling players with family members who have been stricken with cancer has never been the topic of a breakout session. It was my most difficult year in coaching.

I'm a fan of "Friday Night Lights," both the movie and the television show. There's a television series episode with which you may be familiar. The Dillon Panthers have to share their locker room with the Laribee Lions after Laribee's school and athletic facilities are torn apart by a tornado. The head coaches, Dillon's Eric Taylor and Laribee's Daniel Dickens, don't get along too well. In fact, at one point, Coach Taylor slams Laribee's Dickens against the locker room wall.

The teams finally meet on Friday night, and late in the game, Dillon fullback Tim Riggins breaks away on an apparent game-winning jaunt down the sideline in front of the Laribee bench. Out of nowhere, Laribee's Coach Dickens runs off the sidelines and hits Riggins with a forearm, upending the running back and causing Laribee to lose the contest by forfeit. I mean, coaches have done some silly things, and Lord knows I've done more than my share, but you can't come off the sidelines and tackle somebody. That's a no-no in any league. It would be like you racing out of the dugout and sticking a leg out and tripping a runner from the opposing team who was heading home with the go-ahead run. You don't do that. You may have been frustrated enough to consider it at times. I know I have. But you don't do it. It violates the ethos of the high school game, which is fair play rules the day.

Anyway, after the football game, Coach Taylor basically says to Coach Dickens from Laribee, "What the heck were you thinking?" And Dickens says something like, "My wife's got cancer. She's got six weeks to live. I don't have a playbook for that."

You run into a lot of things coaching high school baseball for which a playbook simply doesn't exist. You'll read about several of my on- and off-the-field challenges in these pages. And eventually, you may gravitate toward doing what I call "coaching the whole person." Because you're not just coaching a third baseman or an outfielder, you're coaching a kid who is dealing with life, as well as with ground balls. High school baseball players are teenagers, and teenagers are human, contrary to popular belief. They have human problems.

You ever have a kid come to practice who has visited the orthodontist and had his braces adjusted earlier in the day? You might as well send him home. He'll be a better player tomorrow, and possibly back to near normal, but two hours after getting his braces adjusted, he's hurting. And he's not going to be worth squat at practice. So you recognize that and you don't get on his behind that day because he's performing poorly.

Understand me, we didn't walk around after school holding hands and singing Kumbaya so that our players felt better. We practiced every day, long and hard, and worked our program year-round. All I'm saying is, if you ignore a fundamental aspect of a kid's life that is impacting him and his performance, you do so at your own peril.

I loved coaching high school baseball. Loved everything about it. I loved hitting fungoes and throwing batting practice and developing a relationship with my catcher while I was hitting infield. I still have my metal fungo bat, and there are permanent grooves worn into the old red tape on the handle where I gripped that sucker every day. I loved preparing for games and devising new drills. When I was coaching high school baseball you could have offered me any job in any profession for any amount of money, and I'd have turned you down. I loved it that much. For 25 years I thought of little else. Some people sing in the shower. I tinkered with batting lineups.

Now, I'll be honest with you. I started out wanting to coach college baseball. And I thought a great record at the high school level might get me there. And once or twice, I might have actually been on the radar of a search committee at a junior college or even a 4-year school. Something like 72 guys applied for the job when the junior college down the road from us in California announced that they were starting a baseball program. New field, new ballpark, heck, it was a whole new program, a chance to mold a team from scratch. And if I had gotten the job our family could have continued to live in our same house and my wife could have stayed on with her current job. Our kids could even have stayed in their same schools. But that was a rare opportunity.

That's the problem with most college or junior college jobs. You've got to move to places you probably don't want to live and beyond that, sometimes you've got take a pay cut, especially if you take a job as an assistant. Your wife's got to leave her job. Your kids have to transfer to another school. It's hard to make all that work.

Now, don't get me wrong. I'm not talking about turning down the head job at UCLA or Arizona or Texas A&M or Georgia. But honestly, those jobs probably weren't going to happen for me, no matter how many games I won, no matter how good a job I did. So, over time, I settled in to being a long-term high school coach. I was among the 5 finalists out of 72 interviewed for that local JC job, but they didn't offer me the position. So I was a high school coach for the rest of my teaching career.

You always look back and think about what could have happened. If I had gotten that junior college job, would I have stayed in it for the rest of my working life? Some JC coaches do that. Or maybe I would have continued to try to climb the coaching ladder and moved my family to small towns that housed Division Three and Division Two baseball schools. And maybe one day I would landed a Division One job.

Who knows, maybe I was lucky that I didn't get the junior college job. The guy they eventually hired, another nearby high school coach, was fired after about 5 years. And it took him a long time to recover, both financially and emotionally. I don't know if he ever got over it. That could have happened to me.

What I'm saying, and I don't know who said it first, is "Bloom where you're planted." There are few callings more important or valuable than teaching high school kids. If you can get a group of them on the same page and they accomplish some goals in a team sport, that's wonderful. And in certain situations it can be magic. You can have a significant impact on the lives of a lot of kids. That's not a bad thing.

Truly, I don't know how they get anybody to coach high school baseball today. The liability of working with kids nowadays is treacherous. It's difficult to finance a top-notch baseball program, and if you're involved in summer ball and fall ball and off-season weight training, you're going to need a lot of money to fund all that. I came out of my own pocket for game balls and summer trips more than once. Most coaches do. If you're fortunate enough to be able to raise some money and procure expensive equipment, then you've got to maintain it. And you've got to take care of your field. Baseball coaches spend more time on field maintenance than some coaches do actually working with players. Then you've got parents whose only connection to the game is that they know their son was an All-Star in Little League, and now he's riding the bench. And you make out the lineup card, so the fact that their son isn't playing now is your fault. And you've got to contend with year-round travel baseball today. That makes it more difficult than ever to keep your players competing together on the same team in the off-season.

Today I'm in business, and I love it. It's a family business, and I get to work next to my wife and my son and daughter and I wouldn't trade it for anything. I was talking to my daughter the other day and I was saying that if I had been offered that junior college job I probably would have accepted it and stayed there and coached JC baseball for the rest of my life. And we might have never left that little California town. That is, if I didn't get canned. And if I had spent my life coaching at the junior college level, that would have been fine. But I'd have missed out on working in our family's business. The challenges and rewards and daily roller coaster of running our business has kept our family all close together, and it's hard to put a price on that. Still, I loved the game.

What little I know about coaching baseball I learned the hard way, through making mistakes. I've made every mistake you can make, on and off the field, especially early in my career. Here's what I mean. One year early on in my career I had a big first baseman who thought he knew everything.

Good player. Had some pop in his bat. But kind of a smart aleck kid. Early in the season he hits a double and he's taking his lead off second and I yell at him, "Back one," or something like that, because the shortstop was moving in behind him for a possible pickoff play. And he yells back at me, "I've got it. I know what I'm doing." Well, right then and there, I wrote that kid off. I let him play first, but I DH'd for him every game, because I never wanted him running the bases and talking to me like that again. So I took his bat out of the lineup for the rest of the year. And this kid was a power hitter, something that was rare in all four of my coaching stops.

What I should have done was talk to him after practice the next day. And explain to him why I needed him to follow my directions on the bases. Instead, I just benched him. Never gave him a chance to get back in the lineup, except on defense.

Okay. Last game of the year, I put him back in the lineup. He hits a 3-run jack and a 2-run double and rips the ball a ton every time up. That taught me something. It's like Joe McCarthy said about Ted Williams when he took over as manager of the Red Sox: "If I can't get along with a .400 hitter then there's something wrong with me." (Now, I wasn't alive when McCarthy and Williams shared the bench together in Fenway Park. But I read about baseball history. As Casey Stengel said, "You think I was born this old?")

But that was early on in my coaching career. As you read these chapters, you'll see how I learned. Even a pig-headed, opinionated baseball man like me can change his mind if he sees there's a percentage in it.

Oh, I made mistakes. I've argued with umpires and feuded with football coaches and worst, I've handled kids poorly. I made every bad decision you can make with off-the-field problems. I reacted poorly, dispensed discipline without thinking about the consequences. Shoot, early in my coaching career I was so hyper that I created problems where there weren't any.

You learn as you grow in coaching that usually it's better to wait until you have a real problem than to go looking for them. Enough of them will find you as it is. Here's what I mean. In my second coaching stop in Arizona I got word the week before tryouts that several girls were going to come out for the baseball team. Now, we had a softball team, but these girls wanted to play baseball. And the week leading up to tryouts, I must have had 30 people approach me and ask if I had heard about the girls' plan to try out for baseball. It was the buzz around school, the fact that girls were coming out for baseball. Everyone was watching to see what would happen.

Well, whenever anyone mentioned it to me, I just smiled and said, "Well, we'll see what happens," or something like that. Well, tryouts came, and sure enough, two girls showed up. Nice kids. I knew 'em from school. They had their physicals and their waivers and all their paperwork in order, so I treated 'em just like all the other players.

Well, we're running and throwing and taking a little BP and about the end of the third day of practice, we take a round of infield. One of the girls has got her glove and she's standing behind our starter at third base. And it's a warm day and the guys are feeling their oats and they're really starting to let the ball fly, really cutting loose with their throws. And our catcher comes up out of his crouch and fires one to our third baseman covering the bag, and he snares it and slaps a fake tag down into the dirt and throws to the second baseman. And I look behind our third baseman and I can see the girl standing there and I look at her eyes and they're big as moon pies. She's just frozen. She's never been that close to a ball thrown that hard before, one that could do some damage if it's not caught, and so she just starts easin' off toward the dugout. And the next thing you know she's gone from practice and doesn't come back the next day. And her friend goes with her, too, and she doesn't come back either.

So the problem's solved and nobody's had to be a mean guy and put his foot down. I knew that there was no way these gals would make the team.

Shoot, I'd have played 'em if they could have helped us. But these girls had never picked up a baseball. They didn't even play softball or any other sports for that matter. The idea that anyone of either gender, without having played baseball in their entire life, was going to just stroll out there in the spring of their senior year and make the team . . . well, it was just crazy. It was dangerous, too. You can get hurt, especially if you've never stood in the box against a 90 mph fastball. But by getting my back up and drawing the line in the dirt and making a big deal out of the girls trying out, I would have just made the situation more dramatic and called more attention to it. Instead, I downplayed it and the situation resolved itself. That's what I mean when I say I learned not to go looking for problems. You get a little older, you learn not to stir your own pot.

Trust me, I had enough on-the-field problems to keep me busy. The biggest was that in my four stops in California, Arizona, Texas, and Georgia, I never inherited kids with power at the plate. Don't know why, but everywhere I went, it seemed like we had relatively small kids. Which is not to say that they couldn't play. We just seldom went yard very often. Even in Texas, where everything's bigger, we seldom had a slew of power hitters. So we were forced to innovate.

That's what this book is about: innovative offense. Maximizing your scoring opportunities. Getting guys on base and getting them around to score.

Now, nobody loved solid defense more than me when I was coaching. And Lord, how we worked at it. So just because this book is about offense doesn't mean I'm not a big believer in defense. I'm a huge fan of the long ball, too. But we just rarely had kids who could hit for consistent power. Occasional gap power, yes. Line drive hitters, sure. But usually, that was about it. With the quality of pitching it seemed that we always faced, we had to find a way to get guys around to score.

Now, what you have here are drills and ideas and stories that have useful application for the high school game, which is very different from the college or professional game. A lot of what is advocated here probably wouldn't work in the college or pro game, although some of it would. Matter of fact, our first and third versus a lefty play was a staple in Earl Weaver's bag of offensive tricks when he managed the Orioles. If you're too young to remember Earl, he won a few ball games. Third most in major league history, if I remember correctly.

So sometimes there is some carryover to the college and pro game. The point is, the innovation starts at the high school level, because we can't offer scholarships or draft and sign players. Most of us couldn't, anyway. The high school game is still basically a game of "play who's walking the halls," and there's honor and fairness in that. Each year, you take a group of kids, many of whom you've hopefully coached in summer and fall ball and who have undergone your off-season strength training program, and you put a team together.

This team is comprised of a defense that you hope will limit the opposition's scoring, and an offense in which you hope to attain maximum run production. What follows here is a description of the way we learned to maximize our offensive production. This is how we did it. It's not the only way. That's one of the great things about baseball. There's a lotta' different ways to skin a cat. What you'll read here is simply our way, what worked for us.

HIGH SCHOOL BASEBALL COACHING COMMANDMENTS

You can't beat the game. Understand this or live in misery. If every ground ball induces stress instead of joy, it's not worth it.

At least half of your problems will be off-the-field issues. There's just as many problems with winning as with losing. If you're winning, though, you won't mind nearly as much ironing them out.

Play intrasquad games with live pitching whenever your pitching staff is rested enough to do so. They offer great instructional opportunities and kids who shine in "live game" conditions will make their skills apparent to you.

The ball always finds the weak fielder. If you have to give up something offensively to put your best defense on the field, more often than not it's the better choice.

Find volunteer or hired BP pitchers who can throw hard to your hitters every day, preferably a lefty and a righty. The year Ted Williams hit .406 he had Joe Dobson, an inactive teammate, bring him his best heat every day.

Do things your way. You might as well, since you're going to get the blame anyway if things go awry. Attempt the unconventional if it's your best way to win. If you really care what people think about you, you probably should do something else.

Always emphasize the importance of speed (thank you, Walter Alston). Play the game fast.

Good players make good coaches. Develop your team and your players in the off-season. Work with two or three players individually every day during practice.

Do more throwing early in the week and more hitting later in the week. This will rest your arms for game time and improve your hitters' timing as the game approaches.

When it rains hit whiffle balls with game bats (if you don't have an indoor hitting facility), but swing the bat every day.

Value baseball intelligence among your players. Talk baseball with your players. Tell them about something you saw on television. Show it to them on video if you can. Utilize video at every opportunity to illustrate coaching points.

Teach and utilize the bunt for a base hit as an offensive weapon and use it as a surprise. Most times, though, forego the sacrifice bunt. Let your hitters swing the bat. Apply constant offensive pressure.

Review your signs/signals every day during stretching.

Study the rulebook and demonstrate one rule to your players every day that is likely to impact a game.

Anything you expect your players to do in a game, you must replicate and simulate repeatedly in practice. Avoid wasting practice time on plays that rarely occur in a game.

Build a lineup with a good balance of speed and power. Insert speed at the top and the bottom of the lineup.

Spend a goodly portion of your time working with your pitchers and catchers.

Find various methods to motivate your players prior to practice. Employ a mind-emptying, relaxation period every day before taking the practice field. Players will rarely need motivation to go out and play a game, but occasionally they need motivation to practice successfully, which is vitally important.

Spend your practice time doing what you actually do in a game.

Be prepared to allow for the unorthodox but successful batting style.

Work the off-season: summer travel, fall ball, weight training, and fund-raising.

Play as aggressively as possible on offense and as conservatively as possible defensively. Run the bases every day. Practice team defense every day.

Understand that travel takes a toll on young players.

Relate to your players collectively and individually.

Baseball is hitting and pitching. Find a way to make your hitters and pitchers better.

Have some fun. Smile some. Avoid overthinking. Expect good things to happen.

CHAPTER ONE
PRAYING FOR VICTORY

"Lord, have you forgotten me?
I've been prayin' to you faithfully."

Lord I Hope this Day is Good as performed by Don Williams

I have only prayed one time on a baseball field. That's while coaching. After I quit coaching and my son began playing travel baseball and routinely faced intimidating 6'3" 13-year-olds with sweeping curve balls and heavy heaters, I prayed every time he marched his skinny behind into the batter's box. And then I was mainly praying for his survival. Unless of course there was a runner in scoring position, and then I allowed myself to pray for a little Texas Leaguer.

I don't mean to sound irreverent. But I was taught from an early age that God has better things to do than intervene in a sports contest. My Dad, a religious man and former college football player, often said, "God favors the team with the best tailback." To me, it always demeaned the Almighty to think that He favored one coach, one team, or one group of players over another. I mean, if God helped you win a game, did it mean that he was taking an active hand in defeating the opposition? And if so, did that mean that you were the good guys and the opponents were unworthy people? I just didn't buy it. The whole "pray for victory" thing just felt wrong to me.

But there I was in the Georgia high school state playoffs, standing in the third base coaching box in the biggest game of our school's 35-year history, with my head bowed in prayer. We were getting hammered 6-0. We were at home, it was the bottom of the sixth, and somehow we had managed to load the bases with our no. 9 hitter at the dish. Up to that moment, we had stunk up the joint and had played by far our worse game of the year at the most inopportune time imaginable.

The crowd, which was the largest to ever attend a baseball game in our county, had not given up on us. They were on their feet, stomping on the metal bleachers and screaming for a comeback. Mickey Mantle and Roger Maris had once dressed in our locker room and played against Harmon Killebrew and Tony Oliva in spring training games on this same field. A minor league team called the Rockets once called this place home, and before the advent of cable TV, the dilapidated old ballpark had been the focal gathering spot for citizens in our town. But this crowd easily eclipsed the numbers from those days in the fifties and sixties. From the dugouts to the bleachers behind home plate, folks were standing fifteen and twenty deep. The overflow and late arrivers were guided to the grassy area down the left field line, beyond our batting tunnels, and our Principal strung a yellow rope that held the crowd back and gave the left-fielder room to make plays in foul territory. It was what I had dreamed about and more.

The parking lot had been jammed an hour before game time. Folks parked on residential streets, in yards and in front of businesses, some at least two miles away, and hiked to the ball park. All to see our team play in the state playoffs, a historic school event. It was so loud that the umpires and the opposing coach and I were forced to yell in each other's ears to be heard as we covered ground rules at home plate just prior to the first pitch. Whenever one of our hitters made contact and dropped his bat and sprinted toward first, I could feel the ground shake from the noise.

The folks in the stands, the home crowd at least, and our players, believed in our ability to come back, even from a 6-run deficit with four outs left. Coming into the playoffs, we had won 30 consecutive games, and finished district and tournament play with an undefeated 12-0 mark. We were ranked no. 1 in the state in Georgia's largest high school classification for the last two months of the season. We had pulled off eight wins by one run and several comebacks which defied baseball logic.

Three nights earlier, in our last regular season game, we had been ambushed on the road by a .500 team playing its last and best game of the year. We were coming off our final district win against our cross-town rival the night before, and we arrived late to their ball park and played completely flat. They had a big righty on the hill who was really bringing it. Later his fastball would take him as far as AA. That night we were his meat. He did not allow a baserunner for 4 innings and 10 of our first 12 outs were strikeouts. In the sixth we got two runners aboard and our number 5 hitter, a determined senior co-captain who hit from the left side, slammed a fastball in the alley into left-center, driving in two runs and tying the game. Later that inning our leadoff hitter, a feisty speedster who would receive a Division One football scholarship as a running back, reached third base, tagged up on a short fly to shortstop, and took off for home when the infielder fell making the play. The shortstop was barely off the dirt, just into the left field grass, sitting on his butt with the pop fly in his glove, when our baserunner tagged and lit out for home. The shortstop scrambled to his feet and made a decent throw. But somehow we beat the tag, held them in their half of the sixth and seventh, and won 3-2.

Earlier that season that same leadoff hitter had scored the winning run from third in a district road game when the pitcher mishandled the return throw from the catcher and was slow to pick up the ball. Obviously, we had aggressive, intelligent kids and we encouraged that offensively. It had been that kind of season.

But now we were playing like staggering drunks in a Sunday softball league. At the plate, we chased fastballs up and out of the zone all afternoon and could never mount a scoring threat. Our opponents, who reached the state playoffs virtually every year, were playing loose and easy and scoring against our starter, a talented and tall lefty who would go on to pitch for Georgia Tech. Every time they got first and third, they put on the hit and run and their hitters punched little four-hop ground balls through the spot vacated by our second baseman as he moved to cover the bag on the steal. Several of their hits stopped rolling as soon as they reached the outfield grass. But they sure counted. Our lefty was nasty: He had natural movement on his fastball that broke down and away from right-handed hitters. But it played right into their hands, as their hitters slapped the ball to the opposite field. By the time our right fielder could race in and pick up the baseball, the lead runner would have advanced two bases and we were facing first and third again.

We tried switching up and covering the steal at second with our shortstop, but the one play we timed it right, just as their runner broke, our pitcher fed their hitter something on the inside part of the plate, allowing the hitter to pull it through the left side of the infield instead. It was infuriating. Their hitters were barely making contact and they were pinballing around the bases and scoring.

What I should have tried was bringing the infield in to two steps off the grass and allowing their trail runner to steal second uncontested. Our middle infielders could then charge the weak ground ball without having to worry about the steal, freeze the lead runner at third, and then throw to first for the out. Why didn't I try it? That's a danged good question. Instead, I stood in our dugout helplessly watching little seeing eye singles beat us.

In the top of the third our left fielder dropped a very catchable, routine fly ball that allowed two runs to score and extend the inning. We were jerky, nervous, and disoriented. The team on the field was simply unrecognizable from the team that had won 30 straight and risen to the top spot in Georgia high school baseball. How could we play this badly, I thought?

It was partly my fault, maybe mostly my fault. Every baseball team at every level takes its emotional pitch, tenor, and cue from its coach or manager, and I had behaved the entire day like a man headed to the gallows. Why did I act this way? I have no idea. I wanted to win this game more than anything in the world, and I thought we would if we played our brand of baseball. You don't win 30 straight at any level of baseball without excellent starting pitching and some intelligent, capable players. But somehow I had convinced myself that this game was different, and I got a terrible case of the heebie-jeebies. The game was scheduled for 4 pm, and our players usually reached the field by about 2 o'clock. Instead of letting them hang around the locker room and listen to music, or head down the street for a Slurpee, I had them all dress and hit the field by 2:15. After a short throwing session, we took infield . . . an hour and a half before game time.

Our first baseman, a 6' 6", 210 pounder who would sign a basketball scholarship with North Carolina State, was stumbling over his cleats and booting balls left and right. Now this was an outstanding athlete, a graceful, powerful kid who was good enough to step into the lineup the first day after basketball season ended his sophomore year. (The kid who got sent to the bench when hoops was over and our first baseman joined the team was extremely unhappy, and so was one of our coaches. But we'll get to that later. One thing I'll tell you right now. There are only nine spots out there, and you can't make everybody happy. There are intelligent ways to deal with that, though, and it behooves you to learn them and get kids in the game, especially kids who are not everyday starters. Again, we'll talk about who to keep and who to play and how to deploy them shortly.)

Why I was so nervous, I have no idea, but obviously my players were feeding off my vibrations, and their play reflected my state of mind. After pre-game infield, I went into the locker room to change clothes and I was so nervous that I put my team pullover jacket on backwards. I walked out of the locker room and the sight of me caused laughter among a couple of our players in the dugout. Our co-captain, the same one who had doubled in the sixth to help win the previous game, said, "Coach, you wear that jacket very often? I don't think you've quite got in on right." I looked down, saw it on backwards, and pretended that I had donned it backwards purposely to make them laugh and loosen them up. I would do things like that during the course of the year. Once I had promised to dance on home plate on the visitors' field if the kids won the game there. I admit it was a classless thing to do. But the previous year when we played there their coach wouldn't allow our starter to use a bullpen mound to warm up. Just refused to let our starter throw before the game. Of course their kid warmed up at his leisure. So I hadn't forgotten. Anyway, we won, and I danced at home plate on that field. Probably looked pretty ridiculous, too. At the time, though, I didn't care.

But now, I just looked and felt foolish, standing there with my jacket on backwards, and my players saw through the joke. Kids usually know when you're being straight with them.

Anyway, we played tight, and you can't do that in baseball. You play your best with a relaxed and calm, confident approach. Somehow I had forgotten that.

After my short but sincere prayer, our no. 9 hitter, who was down to his last strike and facing an 0-2 count, stepped back in the box. What their senior righty didn't know was that he was our leading hitter, and came into the game batting a legit .447. What was he doing in the 9 spot? We'll get to that shortly, too.

The kid on the hill was being recruited by every D1 college in the Southeast. Had an angry fastball and knew how to pitch. But he looked at our no. 9 hitter, glanced at the bases loaded with Wildcats, and grooved a fastball. Our kid connected and the ball ascended into left field. With two outs, the runners were off.

The ball sounded good on contact and I thought it had a chance as it sailed skyward on a line over the shortstop's head. The left fielder turned his back and sprinted away from home plate and then slowed as the baseball cleared the left-field fence by 15 feet. Pandemonium ensued. A grand slam with two outs in the bottom of the sixth. Our kids busted out of the dugout like wild horses to greet our hitter at the plate. A game that had been completely lopsided was now 6-4, and we had Mr. Momentum wearing our color jersey.

I was in a state of grateful shock. I said "Thank you, God," and looked up just in time to shake my hitter's hand as he crossed the third base bag and headed for home. In the bottom of the seventh, we scored the tying run on a balk with two outs and two strikes on the hitter, sending the game into extra innings.

Our no. 9 hitter, who had delivered the grand slam, went on to play receiver at a college in Tennessee, then joined the military. Later, he would lead a mission in Afghanistan in which a IED discharged unexpectedly, killing and wounding several of his fellow soldiers. From what I understand, several of the survivors lost limbs, and our guy was one of the few participants to walk away with his body intact. Now that's a situation that calls for prayer. Baseball is just a game.

CHAPTER TWO
IT DON'T COME EASY

"It's been a long, uphill climb."

Middle Aged Crazy as performed by Jerry Lee Lewis

I've been where you are. I've stood in the third base coaching box with fans and parents yelling at me, disgust and anger in their voices. One year I worked a lot of extra hours and conducted numerous post-practice individual sessions with a sophomore who had earned a spot on the varsity. He wasn't starting, but he had potential and he loved the game, and heck, in those days I'd hit ground balls after practice to a pet goat if it was interested in contributing to our team.

Anyway, I gave this kid a world of time and effort. Nice kid. Dad was a piece of work, though. We get about halfway through the season and the kid still isn't starting. I'm moving him up and down to get him games with the JV, but he hasn't cracked the varsity lineup. He's not ready. But the Dad doesn't buy it. So one night we're hosting a district opponent under the lights and I wave a runner around third and try to score him on a single to left with two outs. I know it's going to be a close play, and the ball was hit sharply and got to the outfielder in a hurry, but hey, there's two outs and we got to get the baserunner home. Well, the left fielder comes dashing in and picks up the ball and crow hops and throws a dart to their catcher. It never gets 5 feet off the ground. The catcher takes the throw and meets our guy sliding in and our guy is out by two or three feet. Not a real close play, but in that situation, I think you've got to try to score most of the time. And we'll talk about that momentarily.

Well, the ump calls our baserunner out, and I'm walking back to the dugout, and the next thing you know I see the sophomore's Dad hollering at the backstop, "That's stupid baseball! Those are some sorry tax dollars at work. I can't believe how bad that was." I mean he's really giving me the razzberry and you can hear him all over the ballpark. Needless to say, I was angry. Was I sorry I had spent all that extra time with his kid? Maybe, yeah, at that moment. My point is, you can't please everybody. And if you expect a lot of parental gratitude or public acclaim or even recognition within your school about all your hard work and accomplishments, you're expecting something that's probably not going to happen.

I've stood in the dugout and watched helplessly as our team got 10-run ruled and sent to the house in five short innings. I've endured losing streaks, and years when we had no pitching. I've fought with football coaches over players, coaches who wanted their kids to run track in the spring rather than play baseball; coaches who were jealous of our success and tried to minimize our budget and derail our program; coaches who blamed me because Johnny didn't want to play football, only baseball.

I've also coached teams that knew how to win and would not accept defeat. Teams that won games they never should have won, teams that played so far beyond their native ability that they seemed guided by higher powers. I've had the fans and parents pat me on the back, tell me what a great job I was doing. What they were really saying was, "My kid is enjoying success, he's hitting third, he's happy, and so I'm happy." I learned the hard way to take it all with a grain of salt and stick to my guns.

I've coached some remarkable players. Position players taken high in the draft who went on to professional careers; players who signed collegiately and starred in the College World Series; pitchers who walked to the mound like kings and stalked hitters like jungle prey; hitters who could hit for both power and average and feared no pitcher; confident, daring baserunners; smooth and reliable defensive infielders; outfielders who ran like gazelles and set school records throwing runners out at home.

All that came at each of my four stops, but it took time. When I took my last baseball job in Georgia, I had no idea how bad a shape the program was in until I got there. Had I known, I would probably never have taken the position.

That's the point, though, isn't it? Building a baseball program is not an overnight endeavor. When you inherit a bad program, and few coaches are hired to take over a dynasty (why would the previous coach leave?), you're not going to turn things around in a year, not usually. And you have to teach and coach and work and raise money and recruit players out of the halls and improve your facilities and develop your off-season program and work like a madman doing all the things that are required to have a successful program, and you have to do it knowing that it's going to take a while before you see some results on the field. Changing culture doesn't happen quickly, and it's probably a more difficult task in baseball than in football or basketball.

A famous coach once called it "Belief Without Evidence." You and your players and the people around your program have to believe that greatness is coming, and this belief must be in place before there's any evidence of it on the field. You're like an architect, and you've got to make apparent the blueprint of what things are going to eventually look like, and then your enthusiasm has to draw people around you into shaping that future. Essentially, you've got to have a vision, and then you've got to impart that vision to your town, your Principal, your school, your parents, your fans, the local media, and of course most importantly, your players.

Another phrase I like is "Act As If." That means that you should go about your business as if you are already successful. Pretend that your team is undefeated and the talk of the town, ranked first in the state and destined for glory. Act As If.

One of the most difficult parts of the process, if not *the* most difficult, is maintaining the ability to believe in yourself before all that winning occurs. You lose a bunch of ball games, even a great coach will start thinking, "Hey, maybe I don't know what I'm doing," or "Hey, I'm not as good as I thought I was." Then that self-doubt spills over onto your players. Always believe in yourself and your vision. At times, it'll be all you've got. Protect it and nurture it.

You've also got to keep finding ways to inspire yourself. I looked for inspiration wherever I could find it and it comes in many forms and fashions. I read about Chuck Noll's first years with the Steelers, which had one of the worst franchises in the NFL when he took over the team. And how Noll never got down in the first year, how he always maintained his confidence and his focus. He never screamed and ranted, even with all the losing that accompanied that first season. He just went about his business with a quiet confidence. Noll never doubted that he would win, and eventually, of course, he won four Super Bowls. That's you. You must always believe in yourself and your own abilities. You'll win.

I remember Skip Bertman taking over at LSU when high school baseball was an afterthought in that university's home state. I was coaching in Texas at the time and I attended a clinic Coach Bertman hosted before he had ever coached a game at LSU. He donned the entire catcher's ensemble, and then squatted in that gear, with the mitt, and walked us through everything the catcher does: setting up and offering a target, giving signals, catching the ball and framing the pitch, blocking balls in the dirt, playing the pop fly, throwing to the bases, fielding the bunt, quarterbacking the defense. He was so knowledgeable and sincere in communicating his message. To all six of us.

That's right. There were only six coaches who voluntarily attended his presentation. Now, Coach Bertman is considered far and away the greatest coach of the modern era in college baseball. But back before he won five national championships, back before he had even won a game at LSU, no one knew who he was or cared to hear him demonstrate and speak. But he was not deterred. Even then, he had that vision and that enthusiasm. It just poured out of him.

The trick is not only trusting that you'll win, but getting others to believe it as well. Put your uniform on as if you expect your players to perform exceptionally. Let me tell you something: Kids, even modern kids, who are admittedly more complicated than you and I were, will rise to meet expectations, if those expectations are clearly communicated on a daily basis, and if they are given the resources and assistance in reaching them. Kids are remarkable.

They're also chatty, immature, selfish, goofy, and occasionally mean-spirited. They don't see the big picture like you do. They see what's two feet in front of them, and they gravitate toward what they like and away from what they don't like. That's true for all kids, not just high school baseball players. Here's the thing, though. You've got to reach them. If you're waiting for them to see the world the way you do, it's going to be a long wait. You've got to learn what drives them, and understand what's important to them. You start communicating effectively with a bunch of intelligent kids, players who are committed to the team and to their own individual goals and who play year round and make baseball a priority in their lives, those kids can accomplish amazing things.

Okay, back to our story. How bad was it when I got to my last coaching stop? Well, you tell me. The baseball equipment room was a 3' by 5' closet in the football field house. It contained a bucket of old, grass and dirt-stained baseballs, 5 bats and 4 batting helmets, some catching gear, and a collection of 16 faded Little League sized uniforms. We had no batting tunnel and no bullpen mounds. There was one batting cage on wheels.

Most importantly, we had no field. Well, I take that back. We had a field behind the school, but it was used for physical education classes, so students tromped on it all day. The grass was flinty and thin and brown, like an unkempt lawn.

Worse, the swampy grounds behind the backstop, owned by a local realty company, were full of mud holes, pointy palmetto plants and pigmy rattlers. We had to station a player behind each side of the backstop during practice to retrieve the balls that could be saved. Hundreds of good baseballs rotted in those woods because it was unsafe to send kids in after them.

The infield was made of sand, not clay, the only sand infield I had ever seen. The ball would hit and just stick in the sand, not bounce. To get a bounce anywhere close to normal in infield practice, we'd have to bring the players in on the grass while the catcher and I would hit and retrieve from the backstop, not from home plate.

Our pre-game ground rules meeting was like a summit conference. There was no outfield fence. The twenty foot high chain link fence for the tennis courts stood in left field, the football field house sat in left center, the field house parking lot in dead center, and in right center and right field was open space. A fly ball in the air off the tennis fence was a home run; a bouncing ball off the tennis court was "live" and get all you could get; a ball in the air that hit the field house was a home run; a bouncing ball that hit the field house was a ground rule double; a ball to right or right center, which could roll 700 feet and through the nearby street, was also all you could get. It was like when you were a kid playing sandlot football, and you said, "Okay, the blue Buick is out of bounds and the tree down there is the goal line." Today there's a brand new ballpark on school property, and nobody is allowed to walk on it during the day.

We played the first three games of my first season using this home field before our Principal pulled some strings and got our home games moved to an ancient ballpark owned by the city. This municipal facility was utilized mainly for Pop Warner football games on the football field adjacent to the right field line. There were no bleachers, so fans had to stand or bring their own chairs. There were holes in the chain link fence surrounding the place, where you could squeeze through, so you couldn't lock the place up, and a couple of local golfers used the outfield for a practice range every evening. There were large golf divots from the left field foul line to right centerfield. There were also big gopher-sized holes in the outfield. I never knew what from.

The scoreboard was a black relic from another age and it was constantly going out. The first year we played there we frequently kept score by having a volunteer monitor a volleyball-style flip sign, where you turned the numbers over like flash cards on ringers. The field had lights atop ancient creosote poles, but they were dim at best, and even with a new Rawlings it was hard to pick up the ball. There was an ancient locker room and concession area onsite, but we weren't allowed to use it. The players had to dress at the field house at school, then grab a ride to the stadium, which was about three miles away. Since school was not yet out when practice began, kids were constantly getting blocked in by other cars and had to sit in their own cars and wait until school was over before they could leave the parking lot and drive down to practice.

Beyond the centerfield fence was a small ditch and a patch of woods. Each night at dusk a small fire would illuminate two or three tents in the woods where homeless folks had set up camp. There was one bathroom in the stadium for everybody, a concrete affair with a toilet and sink. No mirror, no soap dish, no paper towel dispenser. One Saturday morning I arrived early to set up for a weekend practice, opened the bathroom door to have a pee, and found a man lying on the floor. He had a long, grey beard and he smelled like a brewery. He looked up and moaned and I just backed away and went and peed behind the building.

A canal-like waterway ran through town about three city blocks away, and a steady breeze blew out toward right center and dead right field all day and all night. When the field hadn't been mowed, you could stand near third base and watch the grass bend in the wind from left field to right. It was like playing on an open prairie. We never got much rain, but fog from the nearby water frequently ended practice and disrupted games. Fog so dense that a centerfielder could not see a fly ball coming toward him until it landed a few feet away. Fog so thick a pitcher could not make out a batter 60 feet away and vice-versa. We had more games fogged out than rained out.

The city maintained the field during the day, because we weren't allowed to leave any equipment there. We had no tractor and no drag. The sprinklers would often erupt on the infield at bizarre intervals, with no way to turn them off. We'd be taking infield the day before a game, the sprinklers would suddenly spring to life, and everybody would dash for the dugout, where'd we sit and wait for the sun to dry out the field.

Our equipment had to be hauled back and forth every day, because we couldn't lock anything up at the stadium. Think about that. The only thing we were allowed to leave onsite at the stadium was our batting cage. It was too heavy to steal.

That August when I walked into the field house for the first time at the start of school, after moving from Texas to Georgia to take the job, the football coach handed me a list of 25 or 30 phone messages from other baseball coaches wanting to schedule us. Our team had won a total of 10 games the previous two seasons, and opposing coaches were lined up to play us. With good reason. That first season we lost our first seven games before we finally beat our cross town rival 5-1 at our ballpark to go 1-7. I tell you, it was bad times.

There was no junior varsity program. No coach, no equipment, and no uniforms. I assigned my one assistant varsity coach to start the JV program and coached the varsity alone. The two teams practiced together on the same field simultaneously. Over 30 kids with no batting tunnel and no bullpen. Darkness usually fell before everybody had had a chance to hit live. It was a tangled mess, and I was frustrated, disgusted, and angry.

I had just left a winning program in Texas, one that I had built up over several years and that was on the rise, with good players returning. But we took this job to be closer to my wife's parents, and because the quality of life in the community was better. The school itself was academically outstanding, and we had two small kids who would soon enter the school system. We scraped our money together and bought a house in a good neighborhood three blocks from the triangle formed by the elementary, middle and high schools down the street. It was a good life, except that we had the worst baseball team and worst program imaginable.

Fittingly, the school had no baseball tradition. In 35 years of playing baseball, the school had enjoyed three, count them, three winning seasons, and had never won a district championship or played in the post-season. We won nine games that first year and never won three in a row.

When school ended we started the first summer travel program in team history, and it was a disaster. There was no interest. It was a rural community, and the vast majority of our players were used to working summer jobs rather than playing a travel baseball schedule. We routinely had seven or eight kids show up to play a doubleheader. One player's little brother played right field for us virtually the entire summer. A couple of times our opponents lent us players to give us nine so we could field a team. We played a modified 30-game schedule with no sponsor and no equipment. I bought game balls and paid umpires and spent gas money out of my own pocket, and my pockets weren't very deep back then.

The next August we entered a fall league in Atlanta 30 miles away. The league offered hour and a half games every Tuesday and Thursday night. On Mondays and Wednesdays we lifted weights in the field house while the football team was on their practice field. We received permission to utilize the locker rooms and concession stand at the city facility, and were even allowed to erect billboard signs on the chain link outfield fence. There was room for 30, and that autumn I sold every one of them on the phone to local businesses, hired a painter, collected slogans and logos, and supervised the construction and hanging of the signs.

It was one of the most important things I ever did, that cold-calling. I probably cold-called 200 businesses to sell 30 signs. I had never sold anything before, and it was an incredible learning experience. It taught me not to get discouraged and to plow on through when I hit a streak of folks telling me "No." I learned to find the decision-maker and forget the people hired to keep you from connecting with him. Or her. I learned to talk to people and I learned to be quick. People in the business world don't care about your problems, they've got their own. Now that I'm in business I understand.

I learned to explain things from their point of view, telling business owners how their signage could help their businesses. Most of them bought signs out of a sense of civic duty and community support, and I learned to say "thank you" and wrote hand-written notes to those who purchased them. I developed a thick skin and learned not to take it personally when people hung up on me or acted rudely. Today, in business, I treat every cold-caller with respect, even if I know I have no interest in the product being sold. It's common courtesy and doesn't cost a dime. I may interrupt a cold-caller and cut to the chase, but I do so courteously, and as a favor to the caller, so he can move on to a better potential sale. I tell you this, if you can successfully cold-call, you can do just about anything in business. I am convinced of that.

Anyway, most of the businesses paid in advance, and I used the money to enter our athletes in that fall baseball league. Things were looking up. Our first fall league game came in late September. The players who were not playing another sport were scheduled to meet at the city facility locker room at 5 pm. We were scheduled to play at 6:45. At five o'clock only seven players stood outside out locker room, waiting to cram into my car and drive to the game. We had no phone in the locker room, but we decided to go inside and consider our options. I keyed the padlocked door and opened it and flipped on the light. Huge, ugly Norway rats, some easily over a foot and a half long, scurried along the concrete floor. They were everywhere. It was like a rodent convention. The players and I backed out of the locker room and stood in excitement and fear. I tell you, I was a grown man, but I was as close to crying as I could be. But the bad news was just beginning.

CHAPTER THREE
TO A BLIND MULE, A WINK'S AS GOOD AS A NOD

"Life is very short . . . and there's no time . . . for fussing and fighting my friend."

We Can Work it Out as performed by The Beatles

My first head coaching job was at a consolidated rural school in California. I knew a little bit about the talent level there before I took the job, knew that there were some hard-nosed country boys who could play. Our second year there we got on a roll late in the season. We had the best player in the district, maybe the best player I ever coached. He was a pure country hardballer, born and raised on the game, and he had a beautiful, powerful swing. Great hands, too. At shortstop, he was marvelous, covering ground like a cheetah. He had a great arm and could start or relieve with equal aplomb. More than that, he had baseball IQ. He had a wonderful feel for the game and just never made a baserunning or throwing or basic baseball mistake. Saved all his extra base hits for pressure situations with runners on board. *That* kind of kid.

Behind this young man and several other talented kids, we strung together a winning streak down the stretch, upset the defending state champions 8-3 at our place, and qualified for the school's first playoff appearance in 22 years. The school hosted a pep rally just for the baseball team (imagine that!). The community was behind us, and crowds were large and loud.

The first playoff game was at our home field. Our opponent was a long-time baseball powerhouse that had won two state titles in the last five years and was coached by a good baseball man who would go on to become the head coach at a college in was then known as the Pac-10.

They jumped on our starter, a hard-throwing rightie who would eventually pitch for Cal State Fullerton, with three runs in the top of the first. We held a quick team meeting in front of the dugout after that half inning and the message was loud and clear: "No more." Our pitcher settled in, and our offense slowly crept back into the game, posting a run in three separate innings. No score for either side in the seventh. We go to and leave the eighth inning knotted at 3. We hold them in the top of the ninth. Still 3-3.

We were battling against a reliever who had a great knuckle-curve that moved down and away from right-handed hitters. It was his out pitch and it had great movement, sometimes even winding up in the dirt and short hopping the catcher as our hitters flailed at it. It was good enough to earn him a Division One offer. If he got behind in the count, he went to the knuckle curve and usually got a swinging strike.

He retired our no. 8 and 9 hitters in the bottom of the ninth. Game's still tied at 3. So our leadoff hitter comes up with two down and nobody on and singles to center. He can run. And our no. 2 hitter has struggled all day against the knuckle curve. So first pitch, I send the baserunner. He beats the throw to second. Winning run is now at second. What are our chances if we wait for a base hit to drive us in? Slim and none, I think, and Slim just left town, so I send our baserunner again on the next pitch. Takes third on a close play.

He could have been thrown out. Could have stumbled, gotten a bad jump, or just plain not made it. It could have ended the inning, and violated the classic offensive baseball strategy that you never make the first or last out of an inning at third. Why send him, then, in that situation, when he can score from second just as easily on a base hit? Is it bad baseball?

Maybe. Probably. But here's what I'm thinking. It's high school baseball, not the major leagues. You're playing the odds, like third base coaches at all levels. But in stealing third with two outs, you're hoping for a bad throw from the catcher or a misplay by the third baseman that can allow you to keep propelling your arm and wave your runner in. Or, you're hoping your baserunner will steal third successfully, and then score from third in the same at bat on a passed ball or wild pitch. Or what if you steal third and later in the same at bat your hitter tops a slow roller and the shortstop comes in and has to barehand the ball and go to first for the out. That's a lot of pressure on their shortstop to make a tough play, especially when he can see the winning run heading down the line to the plate.

Or . . . you can do what we did when we got him to third. Mark this down under "It's better to be lucky than good." Our leadoff hitter has singled and stolen second and third on two consecutive pitches, right? The count is 1-1. I leaned over and told him, "Aaron, we're going for it on the next pitch." He looks at me and nods. He knew I meant steal home when I said "going for it," because we practiced stealing home with him and a few other kids fairly often. What I learned talking to Aaron a month later is that to a blind mule, a nod is as good as a wink. We'll get to that.

I give our hitter the "take sign," then I make sure that I've got the attention of both the hitter and our baserunner, standing beside me with one foot on the bag, and I give the steal of home sign. Yes, that's right. We're going to try to steal home with two outs in the bottom of the ninth in our school's first playoff game in 22 years.

Think my heart wasn't in my dadgummed throat? I could feel my chest pounding. What if he's thrown out by five feet and I look like a fool?

Well, that can happen. And you've got to be prepared to live with it if it does. So why call for the steal of home, instead of waiting for a base hit from our no. 2 hitter? Several reasons. One, their pitcher was getting stronger, not weaker. Baserunners were scarce. We weren't likely to get a runner that close to home anytime soon. So we had to maximize our opportunity. Secondly, the hitter at the plate was struggling. Really struggling. He hadn't smelled a base hit all day and he looked overmatched on his first swing at this at bat. I simply had no confidence that he could make contact, much less drive the runner home. Thirdly, and perhaps most importantly, the pitcher's money pitch, which he went to almost invariably in tough spots, the knuckle curve, moved so much that it occasionally short-hopped the catcher. And I was hoping for a pitch that the catcher couldn't handle cleanly to increase our runner's chances at the plate. Fourthly, their kid hadn't walked anybody in three innings, so even with our best hitter on deck, I couldn't hope for a walk that could get our no. 3 hitter to the plate. Lastly, the pitcher was using a windup instead of working from the stretch, and he hadn't held us close or looked at us over there at third prior to starting his motion. And his motion wasn't particularly quick. And our kid could really run.

Now, I didn't have time to think all those things, one at a time, slowly and deliberately. But when you coach third, and I recommend as a head coach that you actually work the third base coaching box every game, you add these things up almost unconsciously as the game progresses. Each game is different, and has its own tempo and pace. But if you feel the game happening and get a sense of its rhythm, sometimes you can make a call that gives your club an advantage. But you have to be attuned to all this before the play. It's the sixth sense you develop that allows you to know when a pitcher is about to throw a breaking ball, so you can give your baserunner the steal sign, a breaking pitch being easier to run on. It's developing a feel for when to wave a runner and when to hold him up. It's knowing the game and your players and when your starting pitcher has had enough and when you should let him try to finish the job himself. You have to watch every single thing that happens on the field and be ready in advance to make a call. Or, sometimes you run into a young Nolan Ryan who blows all your hitters down and you never get a baserunner to wave around. I've had that happen, too. That's baseball. Every game is different.

Anyway, the count is 1-1, Aaron gets a seriously healthy primary lead, their pitcher toes the rubber, and our kid takes off for home. It's broad daylight, there's no hiding him, and the pitcher sees him speeding down the line out of the corner of his eye. Our hitter is holding his ground in the batter's box, waiting until the last moment before opening up with his front foot and giving Aaron a part of the plate to slide to. The crowd noise swells during the pitcher's windup as Aaron advances down the line. When it becomes evident that we're trying to steal home, the noise peaks in a crescendo, then dies; it was as if the entire ballpark is holding its collective breath. Above the clamor, a woman standing by the backstop screams in anticipation. A loud scream. It was a scream of excitement and impending action, a scream that said, "They're going for it all right here. Whatever's going to happen in this game, this is the moment that will make or break it." It was a primal, primitive vocal release. I hear the scream as Aaron sails down the line, churning for home, but file it away. It wasn't until two days later, when my adrenaline stopped pumping, that I replayed the scene and heard that scream again in my mind.

Aaron is flying toward home with the game in his hands. This kid could really move. Their pitcher lets go of the ball, and our hitter opens up and gives Aaron a shot at the plate. This is the game, right here. The pitch is a knuckle curve, just like we hoped, and the catcher can't handle it cleanly. It one-hops him in the dirt low and away, hits his chest protector, and bounces three or four feet toward the first base dugout. Aaron goes in standing up and we win 4-3 in nine innings.

I head toward home plate and the next thing I know parents and adults are crowding next to me along with our players. The whole community, or what seems like our entire town, has poured out of the stands and surrounded us at home plate in the soft, late afternoon sunlight. A teacher I work with is shouting something in my ear. The players are jumping in a kind of ecstatic trance. The noise is thunderous. It's an invigorating, inspirational scene. Our AD hits me on the back and yells, "Good call, Coach."

The newspaper was full of our daring offensive strategy. The headline said something like, "Bulldogs Have Nerves of Steal." And the story detailed how Aaron had stolen second, third, and home in the same at bat, and how we had defeated a perennial big school power in our school's first playoff appearance in 22 years.

My phone was ringing constantly. People were congratulating us, wanting to be a part of what we were doing, wanting to share in the excitement. The local television station did an interview with me and took some footage of our players. I was the toast of the town.

Three days later I was just toast.

Oh, by the way, Aaron thought we were squeezing him home. He never understood that it was a straight steal. If the pitch had been handled cleanly by the catcher, he'd have been out by 10 feet and probably wouldn't have even attempted a slide. He told me this a month or so later in the off-season. I said, "Aaron, why would we try to squeeze with two outs? All they'd have to do is pick up the bunt and throw it to first." He looked at me and said, "Oh yeah."

CHAPTER FOUR
LIFE IS A CARNIVAL

"I fell in to a burnin' ring of fire . . ."

Ring of Fire as performed by Johnny Cash

Our second round playoff opponent was, like us, a consolidated rural school, located a long 4-hour drive away. So, for some reason, I got it in my head that we needed a Sunday practice.

Now, we had played the first round playoff game on Saturday. And the second round playoff game was scheduled for Tuesday. And we'd leave school early on Tuesday and travel and play on the same day, so we had the opportunity to have our normal Monday practice. But for some reason I was just sure that this wasn't enough. What if it rained on Monday, and we played on Tuesday without having picked up a baseball since the first playoff game?

That's how high school coaches think, right? Well, I called the Principal at home on Saturday afternoon after the first playoff win, and I pitched him on a Sunday practice. Now, normally, any school sanctioned activity has to be held on Monday-Saturday in most states, and California was no exception. So I knew we were technically going against the rules, and so did my Principal. But excitement in the community was high, and the Principal was happy that our school was getting recognition for a positive reason. We had gotten a bad grade the year before and our teen pregnancy and dropout rates were high, so I think he wanted to encourage anything that kept the kids involved in good activities. Like baseball. So somehow, I get him to say "Yes" to our Sunday afternoon practice, and I call our captains to get our "phone tree" going and make sure everybody knew to be at the field at 2 pm the next day.

The next day is a beautiful Sunday in early May, warm and clear. About 1:45 we're rolling out the equipment and guys are starting to loosen up and toss the ball back and forth. And everybody's there but Aaron, our speedster who had stolen home on Saturday.

At 2 pm we start our practice with the command, "Two with your glove," which means "Take two laps with your glove on your non-throwing hand," and still no Aaron. So the guys finish jogging and circle up for our "Stretching and Signs" period, and I asked our second baseman, "Where's Aaron?" And our second baseman says, "Aaron said he wasn't coming to practice, Coach. Said he was going to the carnival today."

"Carnival?" I say.

"Yeah, they got a big carnival with a Ferris wheel and stuff down at the fairgrounds. He's taking his girlfriend."

Well, now I'm incredulous. We're in the second round of the playoffs, first time the school's been in 22 years. We get special dispensation for a Sunday practice. And he's chosen to take his girlfriend to a carnival rather than be with us.

Now, a carnival in a small farming community is a big thing. Especially if your girlfriend is holding you to your promise to take her. Remember, this was before the advent of the internet. Cable TV and ESPN were still in their infancy. We're still listening to music on cassette tapes. So a day at the carnival was a big thing for kids.

But now I've got to do something. Can't ignore a player skipping practice.

So Monday after school, everybody shows up for practice, just like usual. And Aaron comes walking out of the locker room in his practice gear with his glove.

And I call him over. "Where were you yesterday?" I say.

"The carnival," he says. He's looking down at the ground.

"Did you know we had practice?"

"Yeah, Tommy called me," he says.

"But you skipped practice anyway?" I say.

"Yeah," he says.

"Okay," I say. "Here's what we're going to do. We're going to start practice, and you're going to do some running. Let's say, 10 laps around the outfield fence and 20 sprints, and then you're good, and you can come join practice."

And I start to walk away, thinking, well, this may not be so bad. Missing practice two days before a playoff game is not the end of the world. And behind me I hear Aaron say, "I don't wanna' run."

"What?"

"I don't wanna' run." Just like that. No explanation. No nothing. Just "I don't wanna' run." You know kids. They do goofy stuff like this.

So I smile and put my hand on Aaron's shoulder. And I say, "Look, Aaron, it's okay. You made a mistake by skipping practice, but it's nothing we can't overcome. Just do your punishment running now and you can take

BP with the last group today." Aaron was our leadoff hitter, so normally he hit with our first group.

"Nope. I don't wanna' run." He's still looking at the ground.

I'm flabbergasted. "Aaron, you know if you don't run today, you're off the team. I mean, I can't have you skip practice and there not be any consequences, then allow you to play in the game tomorrow?"

Aaron stares off at the cheerleaders practicing drills behind the gym. "Yeah, I know."

"So you're just gonna' leave it like this? Your season's over because you don't wanna' run? What about your teammates?" I say. "Don't you owe it to them to be on the field?"

"I don't know," he says. "But I still don't wanna' run."

Well, bottom line, I had no choice but to tell him to clean out his locker. Right then. He was a good kid, never caused a minute's problem all season until that day. But somehow he couldn't deal with punishment-type running with teammates and other kids looking at him. Who knows what goes through a kid's mind, or why they behave like they do? I remember when I was 15, and Lord knows I had some cockeyed ideas about stuff, so I guess Aaron's behavior wasn't that odd.

Well, it took about three minutes for everybody in town to know that Aaron wasn't making the trip with us the next day and that he had been booted off the squad. The remainder of that day's practice was a blur. First the Athletic Director came and pulled me off the field and talked to me. Aaron was a 3-sport athlete and he wanted to be sure that the door was still open for Aaron to play other sports. Then the Principal came down the hill and I had to go 10 rounds with him. He was already getting calls from irate parents and fans.

"What are they saying?" I asked.

He squinted off in the direction of the practice taking place without me. They're saying, "Why don't we take the kid that stole home with us on the road trip tomorrow and leave the Coach behind."

I thought he was kidding, and I waited for him to grin, or to provide some evidence that it was just a couple of unhappy parents and fans, that we were still together, Principal and Coach. But it wasn't forthcoming. People in the community were upset. They wanted one of our best players to travel to this game, and they didn't care what rules he had or hadn't broken.

Finally he looked at me and said, "Guess that Sunday practice wasn't such a good idea, was it, Coach?"

"No, I guess it wasn't," I said.

Well, between the Principal and the AD and fans starting to mill around behind the backstop, we didn't get a danged thing done at practice. And the mood was very unsettling, just the opposite of what you want heading into the school's biggest baseball game in 22 years.

Next day, we traveled and played without Aaron. And long story short, we got beat 6-3. Would we have won if we had had Aaron batting leadoff and playing centerfield? Maybe. Who knows?

But I learned a couple of really important coaching lessons through that experience. One, stick to your normal routine. Avoid throwing any curveballs at your ballplayers at the last minute, even if you think it's going to gain you a slight advantage. What did I think an extra practice was going to do for us that late in the season? I don't know, but if I had it do over again, I would just bask in the glow of the school's biggest win ever, and tell the boys, "See you Monday."

Stick to your routine. Kids, especially teens and teen athletes, appreciate repeatable, planned experiences. They want dependability. So provide it for them.

Secondly, I learned to take in stride all the folks around home plate patting me on the back after we dialed up the winning steal of home on Saturday afternoon. "Great call, Coach!," one guy said. "Unbelievable play," said another. Now I don't know that these were the same boosters calling and complaining to the Principal, but it goes to show you how fickle these things can be. Take it all with a grain of salt, both the good and bad, and stick to your guns. You know what you're doing, and regardless of what the crowd thinks, you're in that third base box for a reason.

The player who took Aaron's place in the second round playoff game was a wonderful kid and teammate named Jay, a sophomore who was appreciated and respected by everyone on the team. Despite the fact that he wasn't an everyday starter, he practiced hard every day and pulled enthusiastically for other guys to have success. Jay participated in all our summer and fall ball and off-season weight training programs.

Jay was a country boy who introduced me to smokeless tobacco. Every day at practice I'd see him loading up, and I'd say, "Jay, you got something for me?" And he'd laugh and say, "Yes sir," and he'd open up his can of Skoal for me.

It got to be a bonding ritual for us. Whenever I'd see Jay in the halls at school, I'd say, "Jay, you got something for me?" and he'd laugh and go on to class. This was decades ago in a little country setting, and times were different. I'm not proud of my behavior, and I wish I hadn't used tobacco in front of the kids. But I was younger then, and made more mistakes handling kids. Shortly thereafter, I weaned myself off of "dipping" and banned it from our clubhouse and field. A lot of baseball guys have done the same thing.

The next year I left for a job in Arizona. I had fond memories of the California ball club that had upset the defending state champs and advanced to the second round of the playoffs, providing some baseball excitement in the community for the first time in two decades. I was sitting in my Phoenix-area home one night about a year later, watching television and thinking about baseball, when the phone rang. It was my assistant coach from the farm town in California. He had taken over the head baseball position after I left. He was crying on the phone.

"Jay's dead, Coach."

"What?" I said.

Mike, my former assistant, composed himself long enough to say, "Jay was dating a girl, had a long-time girlfriend. She broke up with him. He went out in the woods and put a shotgun barrel in his mouth and killed himself."

It was my worst day in coaching, and one of my worst as an adult. I called Jay's Dad, which was about the most painful thing I've ever done. The hurt and loss in his voice just vibrated through the phone line. They buried Jay in his high school baseball uniform. My former assistant coach gave me the details on the funeral plans, but I didn't go. I didn't think I could stand it. I should have gone.

The day of the funeral I sat alone in my living room and thought about how precious and tenuous life is. And I listened to Elvis sing my favorite gospel song, *In The Garden*. And I said goodbye to Jay.

"And he walks with me and he talks with me . . .
And he tells me I am his own.
And the joy we share as we tarry there . . .
None other has ever known."

CHAPTER FIVE
YOU CAN'T STEAL FIRST

"If you start me up . . . if you start me up . . .
I'll never stop, never stop, never stop . . ."

Start Me Up as performed by The Rolling Stones

The essence of football is the war on the line of scrimmage. Sooner or later you've got to run the football on offense, and you've got to stop the run defensively. You start with that and build from there. Ask any coach.

The essence of baseball is the battle between the pitcher and the hitter. Nothing more, nothing less. That is 70% of baseball at the high school level, maybe 80% of the sport at the college level, and at the professional level it's probably 90% of the game. The other aspects of the game certainly matter, but you start with pitching and hitting.

Consider your team's last game. Who had the best pitching and hitting, your opponent or you? The answer to this one question will, more often than not, dictate who won the ball game.

You start with this pitch by pitch battle between the mound and the plate in baseball, and you build from there. By that I mean this: Baseball is essentially pitching and hitting. The teams that win consistently, at every level, have solid pitching and talented hitters.

Now, nobody loves 3-run homers more than me. And nobody loves dominating starting pitching more than me. And we spent a vast majority of our time in-season and out, attempting to develop strong pitching and hitting on our team. And if you're blessed with a plethora of power pitchers and a bevy of talented power hitters, you can oftentimes just make sure the bus driver has the directions to the opponent's ballpark, make out the lineup card correctly, and get out of the way.

But one rarely enjoys this kind of talent, especially at the high school level, where player development is so crucial. So you've to maximize your scoring opportunities and minimize the opposition's scoring chances.

Let's talk offense. After many years of high school coaching, I came to believe two things. The first was that our goal each game was to be one run better than our opposition, on that given day, regardless of who we were playing. And secondly, to achieve that one-run win each time out, we as coaches should concentrate in practice and games on anything that caused our players to touch home plate one more time than the opposition.

One Run Better

I know these two goals sound overly simplistic. But let's examine the first concept, the one about trying to be one run better than our opponents each game, and start with that. This is a powerful idea that sneaks up on you the more games you coach.

Telling your kids before each game that the goal is to be one run better than your opponent that day is a liberating, effective, multi-purpose aphorism. If you're playing a team that has superior talent, it tells your team that they don't have to be better than this ball club 7 times out of 10, they just have to be one run better *today*. The lesser talented club can certainly do that occasionally. It lifts your kids up and instills confidence in them that they can win *today*.

In the bigs, you are usually playing a 3-game series, so it's a bigger mountain to climb to have to play a superior ball club three straight times. But in high school ball, you usually only have to be better than your opponent one time. It's probably the only game you're playing that day, unless you're in tournament play and facing a doubleheader. So you just concentrate on being one run better *today*.

You're facing Murderer's Row and the '27 Yankees? We've just got to get Ruth and Gehrig out today, not every day, and be just one run better today. Seems plausible, doesn't it?

Now, say you're playing a team with similar abilities. Repeating this phrase to your players says, "Let's play heads-up ball, and we'll give ourselves a good chance to win."

If you're playing a team that has significantly less talent than you, it takes away the self-imposed pressure of having to dominate an inferior opponent. You're playing the Little Sisters of the Poor, who haven't won a game in five years? Our goal is still to be one run better than them, today, at the end of the ballgame. If we win in a laugher, that's great, but going in, we're hoping at the conclusion of seven innings that we will be one run better. That takes the pressure off and keeps your hitters from trying to hit a "5-run homer." That's why I described this philosophy as "liberating."

I have found that, over time, teams and kids will buy into this philosophy and appreciate that you don't expect perfection, though that is certainly your goal. What you should be able to expect is that on that given day, your players will rise to any challenge and be one run better than that challenge. In other words, your players will *compete*, and they will do whatever it takes to be one run better THAT DAY.

Touch Home More Often than the Opposition

Now, about touching home plate more often than the opposition. That idea sounds insultingly simplistic, I know. But the team that gets more guys to touch that 17-inch slab during the game will win that day's contest.

How many times has this happened to you? The opposition is putting up a crooked number, which is to say scoring more than one run in the inning. Let's say they've plated two that inning already. And now they're up 2-zip in the third inning and it looks like it's not your day. And there's a base hit to left with two outs and they wave the runner around third and your left fielder comes in to make a play on the ball. And it's not a super difficult play, just a routine base hit right at him, but somehow your team defense is demoralized, and it shows, because your left fielder botches the play and doesn't field the ball cleanly. Then in frustration and anger, both at his boot and at how the game is going, he picks up the ball and heaves it without aim in the general direction of home plate. The ball sails over the third baseman's head, short hops the catcher, and bounces to the backstop. The lead run scores easily and the batter/runner makes it all the way to third, where he eventually scores on a passed ball later in the inning.

Well, your opponents partially earned their third run, because they got a base hit to left. Your left fielder botched the play, but let's say even if he plays the ball cleanly and makes a good throw, the lead runner would have scored. What really hurts is allowing the trail runner to advance to third, where he eventually scores your opponent's fourth run. That's a "tack on" run allowed by poor defense in left and the subsequent passed ball at home plate.

Now, it's later in the game and you get three runs across in the fifth and you're down 4-3, but that's all you can muster offensively. How much would you and your team give to have that sloppy error in left field and the passed ball play back, now that the game has turned into a close contest? A lot, of course, but you can't get it back.

So you see, you've got to emphasize to your players, both offensively and defensively, that every throw, every baserunning decision, every pitch, every pickoff throw attempt, every swing, every single play in the game matters, because you may need that run later. Winning, at the high school level, is about scoring runs and preventing runs. On offense, it's about maximizing your opportunities, and on defense, it's about minimizing the opponent's chances.

High School Offense

Now, let's talk high school offense. Shelby Foote, a renowned Civil War historian, said in Ken Burns' Civil War documentary that the War Between the States produced two authentic geniuses: Abraham Lincoln and Nathan Bedford Forrest. General Forrest was not considered one of the era's great military tacticians by the academic community of the day. Instead, his military strategies and techniques were based on pure instinctive knowledge gained from inflicting and avoiding live bloodshed. Forrest was like a high school coach who was forced to innovate.

Forrest just saw the battlefield and figured out what he had to do, similar to a high school coach who sees his talent and puts a team together with the material that he's got. True athletic innovation starts and blooms at the high school level. It has to. High school coaches are forced to innovate, because they have to play who is walking the halls. Bear Bryant said the same. Since you can't recruit, or you're not supposed to, anyway, you have to play the hand you're dealt, and that means you have to develop the players you have. Or create a system that allows the players you are coaching to have success.

Once I attended a basketball clinic and the session was about beating the full court press. One of the high school coaches in the audience asked the college coach and guest lecturer, "What do you do if your point guard has difficulty breaking the other team's press?" And the college coach at the lectern said, "I get me a new point guard." Well, there was a smattering of laughter, but the larger undertone in the crowd was one of resentment. Recruiting another point guard is not an option for most high school coaches. What high school coaches need are innovative strategies, teaching techniques and drills, because new players are hard to come by. We are charged with actually coaching the kids we have, and we better be good at it, or we'll often find ourselves out of a job.

The read-option offense in football that almost all colleges run, that's now finding its way into the NFL? It started at the high school level. Some high school coach in Kansas or Florida or Ohio or Arkansas looked at his personnel, and said to his coaching staff, "There's no way we have the size and strength to line up in the eye formation and run inside the tackles. Let's find a way to run the option, freeze the defensive end, and force the defense to defend the interior and the perimeter. And we'll throw off of it, too." And they did. And eventually it filtered up to Auburn and Baylor and Cam Newton and RGIII and Chip Kelly at Oregon built on that with the no-huddle speed game. The jury is still out, at this writing, as to whether Kelly can win with the same high octane offense in the pros, but the point is, the innovation began at the high school level and filtered up, not the other way around. Gus Malzahn perfected his chops at the high school level, and brought his innovations to Auburn up with him.

Keeping Up a Scare

Back to Nathan Bedford Forrest, who believed in keeping constant pressure on the enemy. Forrest believed in attacking the enemy's front lines, but also outflanking their perimeter and mounting smaller attacks on the wings. This strategy he called "keeping up a scare." I love this phrase, and it perfectly encapsulates our philosophy of offensive baseball: Your team must constantly pressure the opposing pitcher and defense, in any and all ways possible.

Now here we're talking high school baseball, which is quite different than college and pro ball. When you have Johnny Bench catching and professional pitchers doing a good job of holding runners, defending the first and third situation is not nearly such a headache. But in high school your catcher may not have a great arm. Or your pitchers may not yet be sufficiently skilled at holding runners close.

So any way possible, you want to pressure the defense, or "keep up a scare." Remember, in high school ball, the threat that you might run or play aggressively is often as effective as running itself.

I have seen countless infielders and outfielders botch routine plays because they had one eye on the ball and one eye on the aggressive, advancing baserunners in front of them. Think about it. You're playing short and there's nobody on base. A routine ground ball comes your way. Easy play, you make the pickup and throw to first. Now, you're playing short and there's one out and runners on first and second. Both runners are off with the pitch and the ball is hit to you. First, you've got to charge the bouncing ball while the runner moves in front of you, which is distracting. Then, you've got to make a quick decision on where you're going with the ball after you field it. Let's say you think the runners got a good jump and the hitter doesn't run well, so you're going to first, rather than try to turn the double play at second or cut the lead runner at third.

Against a super aggressive team, you've got to also know in the back of your mind that the third base coach is thinking about waving home the lead runner and hoping your throw to first won't be perfect. We've scored a ton of runners from second on ground balls to the infield, even when the runner wasn't moving with the pitch. Ron Frazier at Miami did it consistently. Believe me, if it can be done at that level, it certainly can be done at the high school level.

So movement by the runners, and the knowledge that you're playing an aggressive club, creates extra pressure on you at shortstop to field the ball cleanly and deliver an excellent, on-target throw. If you know before the pitch, though, that your opponent plays station to station and takes very few chances offensively, you can relax and it's a much easier play.

Aggressiveness and Speed

"That kind of speed does things for you: It forces the opposition to play you a little shorter at third base, a little shorter at first. They've got to be faster making a play, they've got to worry about being faster. Lou Brock was a hell of a baserunner, half again as effective because he got the pitcher and the catcher and the rest of the infield all on edge worrying about him stealing a base.

"With the infield shortened up, the hitting angles from home plate become wider. The infielder hasn't the time to cover as much territory on a hard-hit ball. It's by him before he can react. So speed is a big factor."

Ted Williams in *My Turn at Bat* by John Underwood

Here's the rub with playing aggressive baseball. You're going to occasionally get some runners thrown out. And you've got to be able to live with that. Not every coach can handle the backlash. Sometimes you'll look bad and sometimes it'll be downright embarrassing and you'll have people in the crowd screaming, "Now why would you want to pull a dumb stunt like that?" Sometimes it'll cost you a ball game. I've had that happen, too.

You've got to have thick skin in that third base box, and you've got to believe in your system. But over time, you'll score more runs in high school ball taking chances offensively. I believe this. Here's when I came to this realization.

We're playing a first round tournament game against a very solid club, very early in my coaching career. It's a big game, played at the home field of the college hosting the tournament. There's a large crowd and even some scouts scattered in the stands. Again, I'm a very young coach and I see this crowd and the scouts and I'm very concerned that I coach professionally, like a seasoned baseball man. In other words, I'm coaching by "the book."

Our pitcher only gives up two runs, but we can't score at all. We get runners aboard, but every time they come to me on the run at third I fear that I'll get them thrown out at home if I wave them. And I don't want to be considered a bad baseball man. Once we get a runner to third with one out, but I don't wave him because it may be a close play and I don't want to take the bat out of our no. 3 hitter's hands, who is on deck. And so forth.

Anyway the game rocks along pretty quickly, and soon it's over. We lose 2-0. On the bus ride home I realize that we have never attempted to score. Not once. And it's my fault. I had a couple of decent chances to wave runners, but I played conservative.

Shoot. You've got to take some chances on offense in high school baseball. Seven innings games are quite different from nine inning games. Seven inning games, especially when they are well pitched, can fly by. You get a guy in scoring position in a high school game, you better figure out a way to get him to the dish. Or at least attempt to get him there. We'll talk more about this when we get to the chapter on baserunning.

Aggressive offensive baseball is not intended as a substitute for good hitting. What you want is a combination of power hitters and guys who can hit for average *and* aggressive play. Because as everyone knows, you can't steal first.

Nobody loves power offense more than me. I would have loved to have had four or five mashers in my lineup every year and just sit back watch them hack. After all, there's no defense for a 3-run homer.

Problem is, how often in high school ball is your lineup filled with power hitters? Or even if you have power hitters, there are days when the power is off, and you've got to generate some offense somehow.

But no one knows better than me that you can't steal first. Let's say you follow our aggressive baserunning philosophy and the first couple of games of the year you're stealing, putting on the double and delayed steal, taking the extra base, taking chances, bunting for a base hit, and generally making things happen. And you really disrupt the defense a time or two and it's working for you.

Then along about the third or fourth game of the year you run up against the best pitcher in your district and he completely handcuffs you. Throws a 3-hitter down your throat and you hardly get any hits, much less any baserunners to work with. There is no answer for dominating pitching.

AGGRESSIVE HITTING

Let's talk offensive aggressiveness as it relates to hitting. In every at bat, sooner or later the hitter has to swing the bat. It may not be until the pitcher gets two strikes on him, but sooner or later, the batter is challenged to hit his way on. Of course, if the pitcher has just thrown six consecutive balls nowhere near the strike zone, your hitter should know to take the next pitch without getting the "take" sign from you. That is something you talk about with your hitters during your first rained out practice.

But let's say the pitcher is having a respectable day throwing strikes. In seven attempts, he only has to throw it over the dish three times. Most guys can do that. So your kids are going to have to swing the bat.

I believe you'll generate more hits, and score more runs, if you swing the bat aggressively from the first pitch. Running up the pitch count and taking a lot of pitches is a strategy more designed for higher levels of baseball, when a long season wears down the opponents starting rotation and bullpen. I like guys going up there hacking. A first pitch base hit is a momentum shift for the offense. It tells your opponent that you're coming to the plate swinging. Now the pitcher can no longer groove a first pitch fastball.

We had a lot of success first pitch swinging. You normally see a good ball to hit, many times a fastball. Against a really good pitcher, it may be the best pitch you see in the at bat. You let some pitchers get ahead of you, even at the high school level, and for the rest of the bat you're chasing and defending instead of attacking.

Now you want your guys to be selective when they're first pitch swinging. They're looking for a certain pitch in a certain spot and if they are at all fooled, they take that pitch. Same as when our hitters are ahead 3-1 and 2-0 in the count. You're looking for a good ball to hit . . . again, a certain pitch in a certain spot. For most hitters, this means they're thinking fastball, so if they see a first pitch breaking ball, they just take it.

But you're thinking aggressive. One thing that really helps bail out the opposing pitcher and breathe new life into him is when you get him behind 3-1 or 2-0, he grooves a fastball, and your hitter just stands there and takes it. Well, man, what are you waiting for? That's the pitch to hack at. If you let the pitcher work himself out of the jam, he'll be that much tougher as the game progresses. So coach your hitters to swing the bat.

The wonderfully challenging thing about coaching baseball is that your hitter has to be intelligently selective. It's not all one way or the other. That's why intelligence is such a valuable commodity in high school players. If our hitter is ahead in the count like we discussed, say 3-1 or 2-0, it's just as demoralizing and dumb to swing at a pitch way out of the zone as it is to take a grooved fastball right down the middle. Swing at a bad pitch and you've let the pitcher off the hook.

Here's where you've got to talk hitting with your players. And show them videos of major league and college games where players are ahead 3-1 and 2-0, and discuss their hitting approach. In batting practice, have your players *hit to the count*. First round of BP, your hitters pretend it's the first pitch of an at bat. So they're hacking, but they're looking for their pitch. Next round, it's 3-1 and 2-0. They're really coming out of their shoes now if they get what they want, but they take if it's not their spot or they're fooled. Last round, it's 0-2 and they're battling to guard the plate and spoil pitches, put something in play. Hitting to the count is something we tried to do every second or third day of BP.

A Few Basic Habits

What little I know about hitters and hitting I learned from watching good hitters swing the bat. And though their styles may be completely dissimilar, almost all good hitters share a few basic habits.

Before you try to change anyone's swing, assess their effectiveness with the one they are currently using. They may look funny, but if the ball is jumping off the barrel, think twice before you mess with success. Conversely, a guy can look like a million dollars swinging the bat, but if he isn't making good, hard, consistent contact, you've got to initiate some changes.

One of the best players I ever coached, an eventual first round draft pick, utilized a completely unorthodox batting style. He hit from the left side and stepped in the bucket toward first base and opened up his front shoulder so that he wasn't hitting off a firm front side. He hit the ball off the back left-hand corner of the plate instead of meeting it out front of the plate. His weight shift was minimal and because of that, he rarely pulled the ball for power, even though he was strong.

He got started late, and because he stepped in the bucket, and because he hit the ball off the back left corner of the plate, he hit a lot of balls to the left side of the diamond. But he was so fast nobody could throw him out. He had fantastic, quick hands, could hit the ball almost right out of the catcher's mitt. And he had a remarkable knack for swinging at only those pitches that he could drive for base hits; pitches that could be hit, but would likely end up as outs, he knew instinctively to lay off them.

With all his faults, he set a school record in Texas with a legit season average of .567. And this was against some of the best high school pitching in the state. He was a centerfielder and leadoff hitter with remarkable speed. We timed him in 2.97 home to first on a batted ball. Mantle and Bo Jackson were supposedly timed at 3.1 on a batted ball. How is it possible for a high school player to be faster than Bo Jackson? I must be exaggerating, right? Well, you are never faster than you are when you are an 18-year-old kid. Bo was probably faster in high school than he was when won the Heisman Trophy and hit third for Auburn during baseball season. I kid you not, he was the fastest baseball player I ever saw.

Our kid could be in high gear in one step. His senior year he stole 36 bags in 36 attempts, despite pitch outs, throwovers, pitchers holding the ball, pitchers stepping off. To try to slow him down, two teams let the hose run in front of first base and created a mud hole where you would normally take your lead. When we arrived at the park the area just inside of first base was a complete mess. Both coaches said it was an accident, that they let the sprinklers run too long. We just nodded and sent some kids off to find some dirt and filled in the water with dry clay and found a rake and smoothed it down. Nothing was going to stop our running game, even on the road.

Now, our kid had a completely unorthodox batting style, but hey, so did Roberto Clemente! Ever see video of Clemente stepping in the bucket? He bailed big time, but he could throw that bat head. Nobody hit line drives like Clemente. What if a Pirate organization man had told Clemente, playing for the Santurce Crabbers in the Winter League, "Kid, we're going to have to change some of your bad hitting habits?" They knew better. You don't mess with success.

Our kid was just hitting a ton, so I left him alone. Hordes of scouts descended on our practices and games that spring, and half a dozen begged for "just 15 minutes alone with him to straighten out the kinks in his swing." Well, I appreciated the offers of coaching assistance from professional scouts, but I knew what would happen if I gave our hitter over to a stranger for 15 minutes: We'd turn a .500 hitter into a .250 hitter while he figured out the changes they wanted him to make. And I didn't have enough job security to allow that process to take place.

Now, I did say to our kid, "Tony, you get to the next level, you're going to have to do A, B and C to be successful. And you'll have to make some changes. This year in summer ball let's work on getting started a little

Figure 1. ***Hitting the ball where's it's pitched.*** *Set the tee up "low and away" and work on driving the ball to the opposite field. Note the hands are above the bat head at contact, so the hitter is not attempting to "surround the ball" and pull the outside pitch. Note also the powerful "V" formed by the hitter's arms and the bat, extending from the chest to the point of contact. Avoid dropping the hands and trying to pull the outside pitch.*

sooner and on hitting the ball out in front of the plate, so you can pull the ball sometimes." Meanwhile, though, what I mostly said was, "Way to go, Tony."

If a kid is getting the barrel on the ball consistently and driving it, you've got to respect that. Initiating a total makeover on the kid's batting style, especially in-season, is like Tiger Woods getting a new teacher two weeks before The Masters. It takes time to change a hitting approach.

The opposite is also true. If a kid is not successful, it's your job to find a way to make him successful. Experiment and change things around. You don't mess with a kid hitting .500, but a kid that's hitting a buck seventy-five and is capable of hitting .350, that's the kid you've got to tinker with in-season. Travel ball, fall ball, off-season, and even in-season, if his problems persist, you've got to find the changes that simultaneously allow him to be comfortable and to have some success.

Video your hitters in batting practice, and discuss batting mechanics with them. Talk about specific changes and corrections they can make to get better. Find video of great hitters and study and discuss them with your players. Then go hit.

On rainy or inclement weather days, if you've got a covered batting facility, that's golden. But if not, hit live thrown whiffle balls. You'll save your good baseballs and still get a lot out of the session.

You and your assistant coaches can break the team into groups of four: One player hits, three shag behind you, and you pitch from about 10 feet away. Start with hard fastballs, then go to breaking balls, then mix in fastballs, curve balls and the occasional change. Have your hitters call out "ball" (curve ball) or "wrist" (fastball) as your arm is in the release position, and train them to focus on the rectangular window above the pitcher's shoulder from which the pitch is delivered. Work on the ability to discern what is coming by what they see in that window. *If they see wrist, it's a fastball; if they see the ball, the pitcher's hand is hidden and it's a curve ball.* Pretend you're throwing a fastball and stop your arm at the delivery point and you'll be exposing your wrist to the hitter. Do the same with the curve ball and see how you're showing the baseball to the hitter in the delivery position.

That's The Old Pepper

I'm a huge fan of pepper. Nobody plays pepper anymore. Great pepper hitters are artists with the bat. Pepper games, properly played, teach so many good baseball tools: how to protect the plate with two strikes, how to get the bat on top of the ball (play the game so that with line drives and ground balls, the hitter gets to keep hitting; but any pop up or looper, the hitter has to give way and shag. Nobody wants to give up their at bat, and young players learn quickly to get on top of the ball so they don't lose their turn), and most importantly, how to make contact. Simply put, pepper teaches young hitters to get the bat on the ball. Players can learn to switch hit playing pepper. Pepper, if you think about it, is the miniature version of the pitcher versus hitter battle, which is what baseball is really mostly about.

Figure 2. Playing pepper with a purpose. I'm a huge fan of well executed pepper games. Emphasize line drives and downward contact for hitters and good fielding and throwing mechanics for fielders.

The ability to put the bat on the ball is something that most of us oldsters learned instinctively, because we played so much sandlot baseball. Even today I can play respectable pepper because the hand-eye coordination you learn from years of sandlot play never really leaves you. But today kids don't play much sandlot ball. Everything is much more organized. You just don't see that much pickup baseball anymore, which was something we did every weekend and most days after school. And when we played, you'd hit and hit and hit until the other side got you out. And many times we'd play without a backstop, so unless you wanted to run after every ball you swung and missed on, you learned to put the bat on the ball.

So essentially, you have to create sandlot conditions on your practice field. Find a way to get your hitters to see and swing at a couple of hundred pitches a day. Pepper can help you accomplish that. I mean, compare all the hand-eye coordination and hitting and fielding and throwing you do in pepper with your typical batting practice session in a cage on the field. In a typical batting practice scenario, a kid steps in, bunts the first two, then swings at 8 or 10 pitches, then runs the bases and then he goes and shags. That doesn't accomplish what you want.

In pepper, your shaggers can work on fielding and throwing simultaneously as they play balls off the bat. If a pitch is so poorly thrown that the hitter can't make an attempt at it with the bat, the shagger who threw it has to forfeit his next turn at bat. That teaches throwing accuracy. Have your fielders work on their fielding form as they play balls off the bat. Teach them to jump sideways to close the front shoulder after they field the ball and before they throw. This teaches proper throwing technique.

A couple of things about hitting in general that I learned just watching the game. First, it astounded me how often on a swing and a miss, the bat had passed underneath the ball. Occasionally you will see the bat pass over the ball on a curve ball down and away or on a low change, but almost invariably, when a hitter swings and misses in high school baseball, the bat is passing underneath the baseball. We'll talk about what that means in the next chapter on hitting.

Secondly, nobody hits the good overhand, 12 o'clock to 6 o'clock curve ball. Nobody. I learned this one summer at a college baseball camp. Every summer I worked a different camp on a different campus. And while most camps are run somewhat alike, each coaching staff had a unique philosophy and orchestrated different drills for campers, so there was always something new to learn. (If you can take one good thing away from a summer camp or a clinic, it's worth the time and trouble. One good thing about camps and clinics is that they often reinforce that you know what you are doing. You see exceptional coaches teaching things the same way you do, it makes you feel good about you and your program.)

Anyway, I'm coaching a team at a camp at a college in California. The college coach sets up his expensive pitching machine to throw nothing but down-breaking, nasty curve balls, pitches that broke down and away from a right-handed hitter. It was late in the week and both teams were out of live pitching. We play six innings and there was maybe a combined total of three hits. The kids knew what was coming and still couldn't make good contact.

CHAPTER SIX
NOBODY EVER "LOOKED" ONE OUT OF THE PARK

"I'd put out a burning building . . . with a shovel and dirt . . . and not even worry about getting hurt."

Tuff Enuff as performed by The Fabulous Thunderbirds

It takes courage to develop into a great high school hitter. Your hitters must be courageous enough to stand in and hack against hard throwers and pitchers with biting sliders and late-breaking deuces.

We're hosting a tournament my second year as a head coach in Arizona. Two teams are playing the game before us, and I'm standing behind the backstop waiting to take the field for our game. It's drizzling, the balls are slick, and conditions are not optimum. The kid on the hill is 6'6" 210, and throws in the mid-90s. Come June, he will choose between a lucrative pro baseball opportunity, a college baseball ride, or a college football scholarship, as he is a strong-armed, sought after quarterback on the gridiron.

I know the kid hitting. He's a tough kid and a battler at the plate. We've competed against him in summer and high school ball. He digs in, preparing to cover the plate against this monster on the hill. It's raining a little harder now, and the ball is really slippery. Big boy on the mound winds up, and first pitch, he lets fly with a fastball that gets away from him, right at the head of the hitter. The hitter crouches and ducks to avoid the pitch, leaving his batting helmet suspended in the soggy air. The ball hisses through the space between his helmet and his head, missing both by about two or three inches. Everybody froze. The whole ballpark offered a collective "Oooooh," knowing how close the pitch had been to beaning the batter. Next pitch, the hitter digs right back in there and stands his ground. Which is more than I would have done. I would have complained of a pulled hamstring and asked for a pinch hitter. It takes courage to hit, even at the high school level.

One more. I'm coaching my first district game in Georgia and we're on the road against a perennial powerhouse in the Atlanta area. I leave the visitors' dugout to jog to the third base coaching box while the opposing starter is taking his warm up tosses. As I pass our leadoff hitter, standing to the side of home plate, I stop momentarily to regard the opposing pitcher. He's 6'6" about 240, and he's throwing harder than any human being I've ever seen. I watched Nolan Ryan and J. R. Richard throw in their heyday in the Astrodome, and this kid is right there with them. The ball gets about six feet from home plate, then rises and explodes, exposing a half dozen illusory baseballs to the eye. It's unbelievable how hard this kid is bringing it. He eventually pitched in the Yankee organization for eight years.

To make matters worse, their field has a pronounced slope away from its center, which puts the actual pitching rubber about a foot and a half above home plate. This guy is throwing *down* at our hitters. He looked like King Kong out there on the mound. Our hitters stood in there like young men. We collected two bloop singles, got shutout, and took a quiet bus ride back home. It happens.

My point is, you've got to have some courage to be a great hitter. Because the further you go in the sport, the better the pitching you'll face. And facing it is what you've got to do. You've got to go up there and focus and get your hacks in and somehow turn one of those pitches around and find a way to beat the big monkey chunking at you.

Great hitting at the high school level also takes the ability to relax. Repetition is key here. Your players have to play enough so that when they step in the box, it's a comfortable place for them. Your kids have to get at least 200 or so game at bats in the summer, and another 40 or 50 in fall ball. Plus you've got to simulate game conditions in your intrasquad and practice sessions.

Kid stands at home plate in a game in his batting stance, holding a bat in his hands. Look at him closely. Is he comfortable, or does he look rigid, like a statue? Does he appear relaxed and calm, or does he look worried and anxious? You've got to be able to go up there and just relax and see the baseball.

Two quick drills. Before you take BP, have your hitters take their batting stance with a bat in hand, and then have them hum their favorite song. Get that going, and then say, "Swing." The hitters then stride and swing at an imaginary baseball. If there's an appreciable rise in volume and intensity in the player's "hum," he's pretty tense. Do it five or six times until, even though the hitter is swinging full force, the humming sound stays the same prior to and during swinging. You're teaching relaxation.

> "I'm convinced that your subconscious can't tell the difference between reality and dream. So you have to paint a mental picture of your future in detail . . . . You can't do it unless you've imagined it first."

Pro Golfer Peter Jacobsen in *Strokes of Genius* **by Thomas Boswell**

Try this as well. Every day, have your hitters go to the plate with a bat and spend a few seconds in the batter's box. Then have them assume their stance and visualize positive outcomes. Have them close their eyes and picture themselves ripping line drives and hitting bombs and being successful in situational hitting challenges.

Skip Bertman was well ahead of his time with the visualization process in baseball. It's hugely important, and exceptionally powerful. The mind is amazing. You stand there in the batter's box at practice and visualize success. Game time comes, the body wants to repeat what the mind has already visualized. In essence, you've already experienced the at bat; now you're just allowing your muscle memory and motor skills to physically repeat what your mind has wrought.

We'll talk about five hitters in this chapter who personified the five habits of great hitters: George Brett, Stan Musial, Ted Williams, Hank Aaron, and Joe DiMaggio. Nothing wrong with talking about Robinson Cano and Miguel Cabrera, of course, but there's more historical video available on these Hall of Famers whose body of work is completed.

It's a Balancing Act

The first shared habit of all good hitters is good balance. You want your hitters to be balanced lightly on the balls of their feet. Better pitchers will hold the ball on your hitters when they're working from the stretch, primarily to freeze baserunners, but also to cause tension in the hitter. So the hitter has got to stand in his hitting position for sometimes as long as five or six seconds before the ball is delivered. So the hitter needs a position that is comfortable, one that he can assume for a while without allowing tension to spread in the legs and hands. Think Evan Longoria of the Rays, who hits with a slightly open stance, holds the bat high, stands tall and relaxed, and then closes his front foot and strides and simultaneously assumes a more athletic position as the pitch is delivered. Or Rod Carew, who looked like a string of spaghetti at the plate, he was so relaxed.

I also believe that "you've got to go back to go forward." Things in motion tend to stay in motion. I don't know what scientific genius said that, maybe the "apple" guy (Sir Isaac Newton), but it is never more true than in baseball. A hitter who starts balanced, with his weight evenly distributed on both legs, and on both sides, can rock gently back onto his back side, then shift his weight forward with the pitch to generate weight transfer and power.

Some hitters are comfortable "sitting in the rocking chair," or just camping out with 70% or more of the weight on the back side. Barry Bonds is an example. Mark McGuire is another example of this batting style. You look at video of McGuire, he starts with his weight on his back side, and he NEVER comes forward. He just sits in that proverbial chair and swings "up" from that back-weighted position. Bonds, too.

Well, if you have a kid hitting like Bonds, with all his weight on his back side and with no weight transfer during the swing, and he actually gets the same results that Bonds got, leave him alone. But how many of us have that kind of hitter in our dugout?

So I believe in a balanced, athletic hitting stance. George Brett is our pro example. Brett laid the bat at a pretty flat angle on his back shoulder, and he even leaned back a little in his stance, so his weight was probably 60-40 on his back side before the pitch. But it was evenly enough distributed so that he could go back, then come forward with a good weight shift and generate power. Brett hit .390 one year. Pete Rose is another example. You see video of Rose, and hitting from either side, he's got his weight pretty evenly distributed. Rose collected a few hits.

Here's a drill. Have your hitters take swings off a batting tee on one foot. First have them stand only on their front foot, the foot closest to the imaginary pitcher, with their back foot off the ground, and have them attempt to make contact and drive the ball. Then have them stand only on their back foot, the foot way away from the pitcher, and have them attempt to make contact and drive the ball. Then have them switch to their normal batting stance, with both feet on the ground, you'll see an improvement in balance when you hit live pitching. Or, if you've got a short piece of rope, tie your hitters ankles together, and have them take swings with their feet and legs tied together.

You ever have a guy who lunged at the ball, instead of maintaining his hitting stance and simply swinging at it? Or a guy who looked like he was going to fall down every time he completed his swing? These balance drills will help that hitter.

Good Launch Position

The second attribute that I have observed in most good hitters is the ability to get the bat to a proper "launch" position just before they initiate their swing. Now, what is a proper launch position?

In high school, it's holding the hands a little higher, at least up near the chest, because not every high school kid can start his hands low and then get them up in time to initiate his swing properly. They may think they can. But watch high school hitters who start with their hands held low. What you'll see is a lot of swing and misses, with the bat passing underneath the ball, and a lot of foul balls, straight back into the screen. This is what I meant earlier about the bat frequently passing underneath the baseball on swings and misses. If a guy has a little higher launch position, he makes good contact more often.

So it's important to make the launch position at least chest high, in my opinion. Ted Williams started his hands a little lower, but as he began his stride, his hands moved up and then started to pull the bat head through the hitting zone. Lots of great pro hitters are capable of this. Again, most high school players aren't. I watched Miguel Cabrera tomahawk a high fastball about 430 feet this past summer. His hands were low and the high fastball comes blazing in, he lifts his hands as he strides and somehow gets on top of it and just crushes one. Makes it look easy. I haven't coached many high school hitters who can make that adjustment during the pitch.

Now, guys are going to have different hitting styles. Resist the temptation to create a team of cookie cutter hitters. My son was playing on a 12-year-old all-star team one year, and the coach tried to remake the batting style of every player in one week before all-star play began, so that all the players hit the way he wanted them to. The players were so confused they couldn't put the bat on the ball. Faced an average pitcher and got no-hit in the first game.

You've got to let kids do what makes them comfortable, as long as they are complying with our five tenets of good hitting. Open stance, closed stance, I don't care. I prefer to see an even stance, but if a kid can hit with an open or closed stance, I don't care. We mentioned Evan Longoria, hitting successfully with an open stance. Frank Robinson, the only player in major league history to earn the MVP in both leagues, hit 586 homers with a slightly closed stance. You see old video of Babe Ruth at the plate? Pretty good hitter, right? He's got a completely closed stance, much more so than even Frank Robinson. What you see with these pros who hit with an open or closed stance, though, is that they most often come back to even as the ball is delivered. But it's much tougher for a high school hitter to start open or closed, then move to an even stance as the pitch arrives. Can be done, but it's tougher.

"Chicken winging" with the back elbow is another common trait of high school hitters. I'd rather not see it, but I've had guys who could hit like that. Albert Pujols hits like this. Heck, the golf swing and the baseball swing have remarkable similarities, and Jack Nicklaus chicken-winged his way to 18 majors. What you want is balance, and a decent launch position with the hand position. If a kid can hit with an open stance and chicken-winging, fine. You don't mess with success. But you wouldn't teach young hitters just entering your program to use that style.

Stan Musial is our pro example here. You watch video of Musial hitting, and he had the most twisted, bizarre pre-delivery batting stance imaginable. One writer described his stance as that of a little boy peeking around the corner to see if the cops were coming. And yet, each time he began to unwind and swing the bat, he repeatedly got his hands to a perfect launch position. Was able to throw the bat head successfully, time after time. You look at video of Musial, and ignore everything but his hands, and you see a perfect launch position, and hands throwing the bat head into the ball with quickness and force. Let's see: 1,815 hits at home, 1,815 hits on the road. That's consistency.

Most great professional and even college hitters will get the bat to a proper launch position, eventually. That they don't start their hands in the eventual launch position is the result of decades of experience. Pro hitters may use the movement to the launch position as a timing trigger. They're good enough to do it. Your typical high school hitter, though, is well served to start his hands at or near the eventual launch position.

Kids will occasionally come to you from middle school or junior high, where they've had some success uppercutting. Hands are held low, they frequently pull their chin off the ball, front shoulder flies open sometimes, but they're strong enough at that level to overcome all that and hit long, high drives. And because they've had some success hitting for power with that swing, they may be reluctant to change over and start their hands in a higher, better launch position.

Use logic and avoid forcing them. Tell them, "Sam, at this level, guys throw harder, and it's going to be a rare occasion when you'll be able to uppercut and have consistent success. So you may want to experiment with starting your hands a little higher." Once they start their swing with their hands in the proper launch position, usually their other bad habits are minimized, also. The best drill for correcting uppercutting is the "tee and target" drill, which we'll cover when we talk about hitting the curve ball. The drill makes it impossible to loop the bat or "surround" the ball and still make solid contact.

Watch video of Willie Mays and you'll see his hands are down near his belly button level pre-pitch. But as the ball is delivered and he strides, he adjusts his hands upwards. You get a kid can hit like Mays in your program, leave him alone and please call me, because I'll pay to come see him play. Foregoing that, though, starting the hands in a little higher launch position will mean more consistent contact.

Last thing on this tenet of good hitting. In high school ball, more so than in college or the pros, hard ground balls lead to offensive production. With a fly ball, the infielder or outfielder simply has to intersect the dropping fly ball with his glove. But with a hard ground ball, the infielder has got to move quickly, glove the ball successfully, throw it accurately, and then someone on the other end has got to catch it successfully. That's three athletic acts compared to one. The math is in your favor with hard ground balls.

Now I didn't coach "hitting down" on the ball. But if a guy was hitting a lot of pop ups, we'd work on starting his hands higher and concentrate on hitting through the "top half" of the baseball. Hard line drives and ground balls will help you win. And your hitters will catch one on the screws every now and again and lift one out of the park. I think you actually see more home runs in high school baseball with this style of hitting.

A good drill for emphasizing hitting through the top half of the ball is having your hitters hit soft toss one handed with only their back hand on the bat. If they're a righty, have them kneel on their right knee and grip the bat about a third of the way up the handle with their right hand. Then soft toss to them and tell them that the goal is to hit line drives. At first they'll loop the bat, and jam themselves with the knob of the bat, and foul balls off and swing under the ball. Then they'll adjust and get more "top hand" action. This drill is excellent, too, for your freshmen who bring an uppercut swing with them to your program.

One last thing. More kids use more bats that are too heavy than too light. They see Alfonso Soriano swinging a huge stick and they think they need a large, heavy bat to be successful. What they may not realize is that Soriano is strong enough to swing that big stick and still generate plenty of bat speed. You want your hitters to feel smooth and whippy with the bat, not slow and cumbersome. A smaller bat swung with good bat speed will normally be more effective than a heavier bat swung at a slower pace.

Get Your Chin On It

Our third tenet may be our most important. It has been my experience that any high school player that repeatedly puts his chin on the ball will enjoy more consistent contact, regardless of his hitting style or other faults.

Putting your chin on the ball means just that: avoiding moving your head during the course of the swing. By "jutting" your chin at the ball as you start your swing and keeping it "on the ball" through contact, young hitters overemphasize a still head and enjoy the other side benefits that come with this habit.

First, "chin on the ball" helps you see the ball. This is paramount in hitting. It's amazing how many young hitters aren't really looking at the baseball as it approaches. They think they are, but video will show that they are only following the ball with their eyes until they figure out how to intersect it, then they let muscle memory and athleticism take over. You want to follow the baseball with your eyes until it meets the bat.

Ted Williams is our pro example here. Much was made of Williams' extraordinary vision. How he could read the label on a spinning record or detect the brand name on the baseball as he awaited a pitch. And his fighter pilot eye exams show that Williams did have very good vision. But more than that, Williams had concentration. And a very still head. Video of Ted Williams hitting the baseball shows his eyes directly on the point of contact.

"Chinning the ball" starts with picking up the baseball in the rectangular window above the pitcher's throwing shoulder. If the hitter can see the baseball sometime prior to that during the windup, that's fine, too, but we only coached our hitters to watch a pitcher's windup in a "broad view," without focusing on any particular aspect of it. That is, until the pitcher reached his balance point.

Basically, it is the point at which the pitcher gathers himself after his rock step, and before he "breaks" (separates the ball from the glove) and makes his move toward the plate. During this pause, we wanted our hitters to visualize a rectangular window above the throwing shoulder where the ball will emerge in the pitcher's hand. And as the pitcher "breaks," we wanted our hitters to find the arm moving through that rectangle with their eyes. And then we want to look for wrist (which means fastball) or ball (which means curve ball). Even high school hitters, if they are well trained, can get a jump on what's coming by repeating this exercise. Over time, it becomes second nature. You see wrist, it's a fastball. You see ball, it's a curve ball. It's one of the reasons the change is a great pitch, because you see wrist and think fastball, but the ball doesn't get on you nearly as quickly.

As you identify the pitch in the window, you begin the process of locking your chin on the baseball. And you keep it there throughout the arrival of the ball and the entire swing, even staring down the spot after contact is made. "Put your chin on it" and "see the ball hit the bat" are commonly repeated coaching aphorisms, because this tenet of hitting is so vital.

Basically, by chinning the ball, you are ensuring a quiet head. Every golf instructor has a different method for teaching a quiet head. Nicklaus' home club pro, a man named Jack Grout, used to grab a handful of the Golden Bear's hair while Nicklaus was swinging on the practice range to still his head movement. Keeping the head still is a vital component of hitting in both baseball and golf. I'm not a basketball instructor, but I bet great shooting coaches will tell you that keeping the head still while shooting the basketball is an important component of success in that activity.

*Figure 3. **Concentration at the point of contact.** Hitters should "stare down the spot" where contact is made on the tee and in soft-toss drills. Keep the head still and put your chin on the ball, every time, in drills and vs. live pitching.*

Most good hitters keep their shoulders level during the swing. That is, they avoid dipping the back shoulder, which can lead to uppercutting, "cheating," lunging, and swinging the bat vertically rather than horizontally. We'll talk about this a little more later. But you get a kid dropping his back shoulder, or not keeping his shoulders level, it's usually going to take his head off the ball, and make it impossible to "chin the baseball."

During soft toss we will command our hitters to "Get Quiet." That meant concentrate for the next five swings on keeping the head still. Then we would tell them "Stare Down the Spot," which meant on the next five swings you keep your head and eyes locked on the spot where the bat met the ball. Keeping that head still and the eyes locked on the contact spot will assist your hitters in maintaining good balance and also in hitting off a firm front side, our fifth tenet of good hitting.

The Weight Transfer

The ability to hit and throw successfully and consistently depends on a repeatable weight transfer process.

Frequently we will hear commentators talking about a certain quarterback who has such a strong arm that he can "throw off his back foot" and still get some mustard on the ball. Joe Namath was famous for a quick release. Partly to avoid defenders and partly because of knee injuries, he often flung the ball without stepping into his throw. My point is this: To maximize power in hitting and velocity in throwing, one must transfer weight from the back side to the front side of the body. Simple as that. The commentator's statement that the quarterback "threw off his back foot that time" tells you that normally, he throws off his front foot when he can. Which means he transferred his weight from his back side to his front side.

Tom Brady and Peyton Manning and Drew Brees throw a heck of a lot better, deeper, and more accurately because they "step up into the pocket" and then, during the throwing motion, transfer weight from their back side to their front side. They are essentially, whenever they can, throwing off their front foot.

Imagine a pitcher who goes into his windup, takes his rock step back, and then never comes forward to a balance point, delivering the pitch from his rock step with all his weight on his back foot. His velocity would be minimal, to say the least.

Hitters who do not execute a weight transfer will rarely be successful at the high school level. We've talked about Bonds and McGuire hitting off their back foot and not executing a weight transfer. Well they were strong enough to drive the ball without shifting weight onto the front side. A vast majority of hitters need to transfer their weight to generate power, and almost all high school hitters need to do so.

Remember earlier in the chapter when we were talking about balance? And going back to go forward? Here's where our tenets of hitting are interconnected. A balanced stance allows the hitter to go back slightly in order to initiate his forward weight shift.

*Figure 4. **Shifting the weight from back to front.*** *A significant weight shift should occur when both swinging the bat and throwing the baseball. The lower half of the body should generate power in both hitting and throwing. Note the hitter's firm and closed front side and how he has "turned up" on the toes of his back foot. Some great hitters make contact with their back foot actually off the ground at contact (Bryce Harper and Hank Aaron are examples). At maximum production, you hit and throw off a firm front side and shift your weight from the back side of the body to the front.*

The weight should move with the stride and the weight shift will degenerate naturally as contact is made. With a firm front side, the hitter will even "recoil" a bit after making contact. That's why you see so many hitters look off balance when they swing and miss. Weight should never get outside the feet, front or back. So you want to avoid leaning back so far in your stance that your weight is outside your back foot and you want to avoid shifting so far forward after contact that your weight is outside your front foot. Essentially, you keep your weight inside your shoulders.

Contacting the ball with the bat causes a natural slowdown, or "shock" to the weight shift, not unlike the recoil from firing a shotgun. But the front leg must remain firm after the stride, which we will discuss in our next tenet of hitting.

Here are a couple of drills for emphasizing the weight transfer. Take broomsticks, or use bats if you don't have broomsticks, and have your hitters put the stick or bat on their shoulders behind their head with their hands on top, oxen yoke style. Then have your hitters assume their batting stance with the stick on top of their shoulders. Say "Swing," and have the hitters rotate their hips toward the pitch. This will exaggerate the need to shift weight onto the front foot.

You can add variety to this drill by calling out pitch locations prior to saying "Swing," and have your hitters pivot their hips toward that particular area. If you say, "Up and In, Swing," your hitters must pivot their hips all the way around to drive the inside pitch. If you call "Low and Away," your hitters will partially pivot so that the belly button is pointing at the point of contact there. Tell them, "Put your belly button on the baseball," and they will pivot to that location. Make sure the shoulders remain level at all times.

The best drill I have found for teaching weight transfer is what we call the "Aaron Drill." As you may know, Hank Aaron grew up hitting from the right side, but with his left hand on top of his right. It may have added later to his incredible hand and wrist strength.

Have your hitters assume their natural stance, and then say "Swing." Have them swing and then hold the finished position. While they are holding that finished position, check to see that their weight has been shifted onto the front foot, but not so far that they are out in front of it and off balance. Also correct your hitters if their shoulders are not level. Then say, "Okay, back to your hitting position," and call "Swing," and repeat the process several times.

Then, when you are comfortable that a good weight transfer is being effected and that shoulders are level, add the second part of the drill. The players swing the bat on your command, hold their balanced finish position for one or two seconds, then you holler "Swing" again, and the hitters swing the bat wrong-handed back to the starting position. They must shift their weight and keep their shoulders level as they swing back.

Now if you hit right-handed, as most of your hitters will, your right hand will be on top. At the finish of the first swing forward, the hitter turns his head back toward an imaginary pitcher over his right shoulder, rebalances, then takes a "swing back" wrong-handed, working on weight transfer, balance and bat speed.

Later you can have your hitters take their first swing, hold their finish position, then switch hands, so that their left hand is on top on the return swing, and it is a true switch-hitting movement. But throughout the drill, you want weight transfer with each swing forward and each swing back.

And your hitters will shift their weight, especially when you swing wrong-handed. Because you've got the wrong hand on top, it's much more difficult to get your weight to go back in the return swing, so your hitters have to focus on shifting weight in the hips and lower body, which is what you want.

This drill, successfully employed, also develops excellent bat speed, and gives hitters that "swishy" feeling with the bat. You execute this drill back and forth 25 times or so, and you'll like the benefits. One thing I liked to do was have our coaches walk around and give the hitters an occasional light push on the shoulder as they held their finish positions. If the hitter isn't balanced, you'll be able to tell. If he didn't shift his weight, he'll fall back toward his back foot. If he shifted too far, he'll fall toward the outside part of his front foot. Balance and bat speed are a great combination and you are always seeking these two components in hitting.

Part of the reason we named this drill after Hank Aaron is because of his weight shift. If you study video of Aaron, you'll see that at contact, his weight shift is so complete that his back foot is slightly off the ground. That's right, Aaron's back foot does not touch the ground at contact. You talk about hitting off a firm front side with a great weight shift! The man nailed 755 dingers, hitting off one foot. Old film clips of Babe Ruth show the same thing. On about every other swing, Ruth's back foot is off the ground at contact. What did he hit, 714 homers? Roger Maris did the same thing. Now with Aaron and Ruth you're talking about two of the greatest home run hitters ever, and with Maris, a guy who compiled one of the great single home run seasons. And all of these guys had their back foot off the ground at contact.

Now, do you teach that? I wouldn't, though I have had a player or two hit successfully in that fashion. But it goes to show you how important a weight shift is.

What you want to teach is to pivot on the back foot and point the back big toe toward the pitcher at contact. This makes the hitter shift his weight onto his front side. Remember the broomstick drill? After you have had your hitters execute several hip pivots, and then given them hip pivots toward certain locations, call "Swing and Pivot," and have the hitters rotate their hips toward an imaginary fastball down the middle, while concentrating on pivoting on the back foot and pointing the toe toward the pitcher.

During batting practice, if you have a hitter whose back foot naturally comes up off the ground slightly at contact, that may be his natural style. If he's having success, there's nothing wrong with it; if he's not, you may want to work with him on keeping the back foot on the ground and pivoting. It has been my experience that this type of hitter is more often a contact hitter than a power hitter. So if you want him to generate more power, he probably needs both feet on the ground. There is really no explanation for Hank Aaron and his power. Great hitters use a remarkable variety of styles.

Hitting Off a Firm Front Side

> "Hit against a firm left side, but hit from the right side. That's the source of power."
>
> Professional golfer Calvin Peete in Tom Boswell's *Strokes of Genius*

One of the simplest and most important lessons I learned in teaching throwing mechanics to infielders is to turn sideways toward your target. After and even as you field the ball, simply jump pivot to the side, so that (for a right-handed thrower) your front left shoulder is lined up sideways with the target. Then you execute the throw through this closed front side.

Imagine in your mind an outfielder come charging in on a base hit to the outfield to make a play. You see him field the ball with his shoulders squared, then as he crow hops to let the throw sail toward home, what does he automatically do to gain throwing power? He closes the front shoulder.

Imagine an outfielder fielding a base hit and then throwing home while keeping his front shoulder open. You never see it, and there's a reason for it.

Pitchers are constantly coached to avoid allowing their front shoulder to "fly open" as they deliver the ball. Pitchers want to drive their front shoulder vertically, not horizontally. Opening the front shoulder dissipates power and disrupts throwing rhythm. Back to football. Quarterbacks are turned sideways toward their target, and they throw through a closed front side.

This Sunday, if you are reading this during football season, tune in and watch NFL quarterbacks as they deliver the football. And then look at their front leg (the one closest to the target or receiver), which will be their left leg if they are a right-handed quarterback. Watch that front leg as the pass is thrown. Does it collapse and continue moving forward? No, it stands firm and virtually rigid, and the QB throws the ball through this firm front side. With many passers, you will see the slight recoil as they release the ball and rock back.

The same exact thing is true in hitting. One must hit off a firm, or closed front side, and keeping the front shoulder closed is part of that equation. If the front shoulder flies open prior to contact, it disrupts good hitting mechanics. Frequently it will cause the hitter's head to move; it can cause the hitter to lunge at the ball, which of course is a balance problem; and it can cause the hitter to "cheat," which means to start with the bat head before he's ready to explode with the hips. The hips should lead and direct the hands in the swing, and if the hands get out front, it's often caused by opening the front shoulder.

Imagine that the hitter's front leg is the post in the middle of a revolving door in a big city building entrance. The doors that revolve around the post represent the arc of the hitter's swing. The post never moves, but the doors keep circling, right? This is essentially what you want your front leg and front side to do: remain firm and allow the arc of the swing to move around it.

The weight transfer stops at the front leg. This is what makes Hank Aaron's hitting style so remarkable. Aaron had to time his weight transfer perfectly, so that during his stride his weight was moved off his back foot completely, transferred to the front side as he made at contact, then stopped on the front leg. That is why I don't recommend teaching hitters to hit with their back foot off the ground. It takes excellent timing on every swing. Again, Hank Aaron was different. I love the Ken Burns *Baseball* documentary, which talked about a pitchers' meeting before a team faced Aaron's ball club. The pitching coach was going through the lineup and discussing how to pitch each hitter. When the pitching coach got to Aaron, there was silence. And one guy finally says, "Make sure there's nobody on when he hits it out."

I never coached hitters to turn their front foot toes inward toward home plate, in order to establish a firm front side. I think that's overdoing it. However, normally you want your hitters' front foot to be, if not closed, at least even with the shoulders in a normal or even batting stance (a stance in which the hitter utilizes neither an open or closed stance). This will normally help the front leg to serve as the "stopper" in the weight transfer, just as your shoulder is the "stopper" when you fire a shotgun and the gun recoils off your body.

Joe DiMaggio is our pro example here. What a compact swing he had! Find video of DiMaggio swinging (there are some great shots in the Ken Burns *Baseball* documentary) and you will see a completely minimized swing utilizing a very short stride, with no wasted motion, executed around a still head and a completely firm front side. DiMaggio's stride foot barely came off the ground, then he set it in place just like the post in our revolving door. His hands start in the eventual launch position as well. DiMaggio's swing may encapsulate our five tenets of good hitting as well as anyone's. Also study Hall of Famer Paul Molitor, who, like DiMaggio, used a very, very compact stroke with no wasted motion, rotating around a quiet head and a firm front side.

A good drill using soft toss is to have your hitters turn 45 degrees outward, so that their front shoulder and front leg point about halfway between the pitcher and third base. Then have them swing five or six times in this awkward position. Then have them close up to their normal stance and hit five or six more soft tosses, and they will feel the power that's generated by hitting off their normal closed front side.

HITTING THE BREAKING BALL

In one of my first coaching stops I coached a kid who was a great curve ball hitter. Actually preferred the curve to the fastball. This kid did more than hit the curve ball back through the middle or to right field for singles. He creamed it. He ripped screaming drives into the gap and would pull long, soaring home runs over the left field fence.

It was my first year to coach him, and as you can imagine, he was a curiosity at the high school level. I watched him take batting practice and hit in games and developed a dialogue with him about it.

"Terry," I said, "how come you hit the curve ball so well?" "I dunno" he said. "I just do."

Now is that a typical teenage response, or what?

"What do you do differently swinging at the curve ball?" I asked. "Well, when I recognize that it's a spinner, I stop and sit down in my stance. Then I don't come out of it 'til I swing. And I just hit it where it's pitched."

Terry's response, in a nutshell, is just about all I know about hitting the curve ball at the high school level. But there's more to what he said than meets the eye.

First, there's the recognition process. Terry was my cheetah-like shortstop, the California country hardballer who had so much natural and self-taught ability. He understood intuitively what I meant when I taught the team to look for "wrist" or "ball" in the window above the pitcher's shoulder, but he already knew to do that on his own. I'm not sure he was doing it my way, but he could recognize when the curve was coming.

As soon as he did, he "sat down in his stance." Now by this I mean, and I can picture him in my mind's eye, he simply delayed his stride and weight transfer and crouched slightly in an athletic position. He maintained his even shoulder level, and kept his hands back and in the launch position.

Then, when the ball was in range, he strided, shifted his weight, and just blistered the baseball.

So in effect, he had a two-part swing against the breaking ball. He set up in his normal stance and began his normal swing against the fastball, but "sat down" when he recognized "breaking ball." Then he reemerged smoothly with the stride and swing, which was the second part of his attack.

You can hit the average high school breaking ball this way. I know it sounds simplistic and even a little ridiculous. But think for a minute. Have you ever had anyone successfully coach your hitters on how to hit the curve ball? I certainly hadn't. And this worked for us.

We developed drills to teach this style. And sure enough, they transferred successfully to game conditions. It's probably impossible to hit the pro or even the college breaking ball in this fashion. The pitches come too hard and break too sharply and there's too much down-break to them. But you can teach kids to hammer the average high school curve this way.

Two drills. One, your hitters are facing a coach with a baseball in his hand. The coach goes into his windup and shows "ball" in the window above his pitching shoulder. As soon as the hitter recognizes curve ball, he stops his hitting motion and executes a slight "sit" into an athletic, power position. Then the coach finishes his pitching motion and throws a breaking ball (this is easily done with whiffle balls from about 10 feet away), and the hitter uncoils and strokes the ball.

The second drill is one of the best hitting drills I know. Use a multiple-tip tee with at least five hitting cups. Set the tee up against a chain link fence or your batting tunnel net. Tie red rags (the kind you use to check your car's oil level are perfect) in the chain link or the netting where you want the baseball to intersect the chain link or the net as it comes off the bat. Adjust the height of the tee tip closest to the hitter so that he is swinging at a pitch up and in. Tie a red rag "in the alley" in left center, where a right-handed hitter would normally hit a ball if he turned on an inside pitch and hit it solidly, onto the chain link or the netting. Do the same for the pitch on the middle tee, adjusting the tee down slightly about two inches. Tie the rag so that the target is right back through the pitcher's mound.

Lastly, put the baseball on the tee tip that is low and away, and lower that tee so that the ball is in the lower, outside edge of the strike zone, or where a curve ball winds up in the zone. Then tie a red rag in "the alley" in right center and have the player hit the ball off the tee and make it strike the red rag in "right center" when it smacks the chain link or the netting.

In order for the hitter to strike the ball on the tee cup that is up and in and cause it to hit the red rag in left center, he's got to whip the bat head around and get on top of the pitch. And to do that he's got to pivot his hips and put his belly button on the tee tip. With the ball back up the middle he'll use his normal stroke and put his belly button on that tee tip.

With the ball sitting on the tee low and away, have the player start his swing, then "sit down" and assume the athletic, power position we have described when recognizing curve ball. Then have him finish his swing, keeping the hands above the bat head, and drive the ball into the red rag in right center.

If the player tries to come around the ball that's low and away, his batted ball will end up hitting closer to the middle rag or even the rag in left center. This tells you that he is "looping" the bat and trying to "surround" the pitch that's low and away, a common fault among young hitters versus the curve ball. By sitting down in his stance, then driving the ball to the red rag in right center, he will still be leading the bat head with his hands and hitting the ball for power. This is an excellent drill for your freshman who come to you with an uppercut, and it's an excellent drill for your varsity. This is teaching young players to hit the ball where it's pitched.

Keep Your Own Counsel

During my first year as a head coach, I had yet to develop a very good "filter." By this I mean that anything I heard from or read by a "baseball expert," I considered as gospel. Now there are a couple of exceptions, like books by Danny Litwhiler and Jerry Kendall. You get hold of one of those, you can take the drills in the book to the bank. They are golden. They work. Every drill that I picked up from one of their books was practical and produced positive benefits. Those guys were practice and drill experts.

But you've got to develop a good filter and trust what you already know. First year as a head coach in California, I'm watching a junior college game. And I'm listening to everything the coach says to his hitters during the game, trying to learn and pick up anything I can. The kid on the hill for the opposing team has a pretty good snapper and is getting everybody out on it. So the third base coach is repeating ad nauseam to his hitters: "Hit the curve ball to right field." I hear him say this to every hitter struggling with this kid's curve, which was just about his whole lineup. And the coach's frustration kept growing, because nobody could hit the curve ball to right field. At least that I saw, anyway.

Well, as I aged in the profession, I came to realize there are a couple of problems with telling your players during a game to "hit the curve ball to right field." First, you can't teach your kids to hit during a live game. That must be done in practice and in intrasquad games and during hundreds of hours of soft tossing and drills around the batting tunnel. Once game time arrives, you have to let your kids go play. You're coaching third, and your hitter comes up with two on and two out and the pitcher has been struggling to throw strikes, you might form a small rectangular "box" with your hands and show it to your hitter, meaning "make him throw it over the plate," or "be selective, he's struggling," but that's about it. You sure can't teach him to hit the curve ball during a game.

Secondly, the pitcher's breaking ball may start at the hitter's front shoulder and break over the inside or middle part of the plate. You don't want to hit that pitch to right. You want to pull it or hit it back up the middle. So commanding every hitter to hit the curve ball to right field is counterproductive. You want to hit the curve ball, and the fastball, where it's pitched.

Lastly, anything you expect your players to do in a game, you must develop drills for them in practice that teach those actions. You can't wait 'til game time and then holler at your second baseman, "Now bust it around the bag on the double play." The footwork your second baseman will use in turning two is something that you have to work on daily. And you get to game time, you've got to trust what you've done with your kids up to that point and let them go play.

Do you remember your last at bat as a player? What if your coach had been yelling at you during that at bat, saying "Hit the curve ball to right field." Well, you'd just nod your head, stand back in, and do what you've always done.

So keep your own counsel, and develop a good filter. You know what you're doing.

And that's about all I know about hitting the curve ball. Other than the fact that nobody hits the good overhand curve.

CHAPTER SEVEN
BUILDING A GOOD LINEUP

*"Lightnin' started flashin' and thunder started crashin' . . .
Shhoooh . . . white lightning!"*

White Lightnin' as performed by George Jones

An integrated approach to aggressive offensive baseball starts with building the kind of lineup that you are comfortable with and that will, in your opinion, produce the largest number of runs. The kind of lineup that will produce "White Lightnin'."

"Rabbits"

I like to put my no. 1, 2, 6, 8, and 9 hitters in a group. I like to have them practice together, as many of their skills are interchangeable. I want these five guys to specialize in getting on base, starting rallies, scoring runs, and extending innings. I want to work with them, and their backups, every day on bunting for a base hit, hitting to the count, stealing, and running the bases. I want to talk hitting with them daily and make sure they understand that their value lies in setting the table for other hitters. These guys should score a lot of runs.

The leadoff hitter, whom we'll discuss momentarily, is challenged with the obvious task of getting on base to start the game, and then getting on base each time he subsequently comes to the plate. Your no. 2 hitter should have an excellent eye and be a good contact hitter. If he can run and hits from the left side, that's a bonus. I have found over the years that the no. 6 hitter also frequently leads off innings and functions almost like a second leadoff hitter. I usually put an RBI guy in front of him in the 5-spot, and he would often be our slowest player among the first five hitters, so frequently the no. 6 hitter would lead off the next inning after our no. 5 guy was thrown out. If your no. 6 hitter can run and handle the bat and has power, that's optimum.

My no. 8 and 9 hitters' sole function is to get us back to the top of the lineup, any way they can. Your no. 8 hitter should be one of your best at bunting for a base hit and should have speed. You want both your 8 and 9 hitters to consider a walk a base hit, and to be selective.

Hide an excellent fastball hitter, one who can run, in the 9-spot. Here we come full circle back to the first story in this book, the one about my no. 9 hitter who answered my prayer in the playoff game with a grand slam. That young man, the one who hit the slam, led our team in hitting that year. Yes, our leading hitter batted in the 9-spot.

So, if he was that good a hitter, why didn't I bat him higher in the lineup? Well, in the 3 or 4 or even 6-spot in the lineup, he wouldn't have seen nearly as many good pitches to hit, and probably wouldn't have hit over .400. He was a little stiff in his approach at the plate, and struggled with off-speed pitches. But he was an excellent athlete with great speed and great hand eye coordination, and he was a really good fastball hitter. Well, sitting in that 9-spot, he saw lots of fastballs.

How many times, when the tail end of your order was due up, have you heard an opposing coach yell to his battery and his team as they took the field for an inning, "Okay, 7-8-9 here!" That's code for "these are the other team's weakest hitters. Let's throw fastballs over the plate and they'll get themselves out."

So seeing a lot of fastballs, and a lot of good pitches to hit, upped his average. He was also extremely adept at bunting for a base hit, and did so successfully eight or nine times that season. So that upped his batting average considerably. As they say, "It'll look like a line drive in the box score." You get a guy in the 9-spot who can bunt for a base hit and everybody's safe and the inning continues as you bring your leadoff hitter back to the plate, you've really got something going offensively.

Now, we coached him to understand his role. I told him, "Mark, with your ability you could be hitting higher in the lineup. You and I both know that. But our 9-hole hitter is as valuable to us as anybody in the lineup, maybe more so than some spots. And you know that we have traditionally chosen a very talented, fast player to hit in that spot. Now, how do you feel about hitting there?"

His response was perfect, "Coach," he said, "I know that's what we do and I think I can hit well there." As the season progressed, we took time out during team meetings to applaud Mark and his contributions to the team. And to announce that, in the 9-spot, Mark was leading the team in hitting. By the end of the year, the 9-spot was the only place he wanted to hit, and he would have objected, or at least questioned our wisdom, had we tried to move him up in the lineup.

By emphasizing Mark's contribution in the 9-spot to the team, we were in effect telling them, "Every spot in the lineup is important, and it's not where you hit, it's what you do when you come up that counts."

Those 8 and 9 guys are just like surrogate leadoff hitters. They should be selective and find a way to get on base. We tell these five guys, hitting in the 1, 2, 6, 8, and 9-spots, that they are all "leadoff hitters." Occasionally we would switch them around, especially early in the season, so they could understand the role that their counterparts were playing. We would move everybody down one spot: The leadoff hitter would hit sixth, the no. 2 hitter would hit eighth, the no. 6 hitter would hit ninth, the no. 8 hitter would lead off, and our no. 9 hitter would move up and hit in the 2-spot.

Early in the season we often experimented with swapping the no. 1 and 6 hitters to see who handled the leadoff role better.

Building a Good Lineup

I believe it is healthy to try different batting lineups. As you progress into the heart of your schedule and into district play, then I think it is helpful to decide on an everyday batting order. Players, and most young people, like order and dependability and repeatable experiences. Compared with their chaotic teenage lives, sameness in the batting order and practice regimen can lend a sense of comfort.

Building a good lineup is part art and part science. Traditional thinking is your best on-base percentage guy that can run should lead off, you utilize a guy who can handle the bat in the 2-hole, your best overall hitter should hit third, the guy most likely to hit the ball out of the yard should hit clean up, your best pure RBI guy should hit fifth. And so on.

The Leadoff Hitter

Well, that's all true enough. But what if your best on-base percentage guy who can run, your natural leadoff hitter, does not flourish in the leadoff spot? Not everybody can hit leadoff. A leadoff hitter has got to react to the first pitch thrown in the game, and is expected to hit the ball hard and get on base, and then make something happen when he gets there. It's a lot of pressure, and not everybody can do it.

Here's where knowing your kids is important. Who's the most confident, brash, competitive, and cocky kid you have? He doesn't have to be a mouthy guy, but he's got to be oozing with a competitive streak. That's usually a good candidate for the leadoff spot. Over the years I have found that multi-sport athletes frequently make good leadoff hitters, as they often have an extra slice of courage and verve and they frequently enjoy large crowds, as opposed to being intimidated by them.

Ideally, you want a guy who can both hit and run. One without the other diminishes the value of a leadoff man. If you don't have a player with both skills, you want to err on the side of the better hitter, because as we've already said, you can't steal first. Paul Mainieri at LSU got a lot of mileage this past year out of a left-handed hitting leadoff hitter who had gap power. Not his fastest player, but it was a guy who could occasionally start a ball game by ripping a double into the alley. Mainieri's fastest guy, a true freshman also hitting from the left side, hit second.

Now if the true freshman had been a better hitter, Mainieri probably would have wanted to hit him in the leadoff spot. But the freshman wasn't ready for that role, I don't think, and so Mainieri went with the better hitter in the leadoff spot. It allowed his freshman hitting in the 2-spot to develop slowly during the non-conference season, and by SEC tournament time, he was one of the Tigers best offensive threats. And he can fly as well. Wouldn't surprise me to see him in the leadoff role in the near future.

Point is, Mainieri went with the better hitter, even thought he had more speed in the 2-hole.

I cannot overemphasize how important it is to develop a good leadoff man. As you well know, getting him on base and getting him around to score early in the game to give you a lead gives your ball club tremendous confidence and allows greater coaching flexibility for you. It's a lot easier to call for a steal of third with one out if you're up 2-zip than if you're down by the same score.

The perfect leadoff hitter is, first and foremost, great at reaching base, an excellent hitter with a fine sense of the strike zone, an outstanding baserunner with good speed, and also someone who can bunt for a base hit. That's a lot to ask in one player, isn't it? But that's why your leadoff man is so valuable.

A consummate leadoff hitter loves to come to the plate and loves to run the bases. He embraces the role. And no matter how good a hitter he is, and you want a danged good hitter in the leadoff spot, you've got to impress upon him that his main goal is to reach base. Say, "Charlie, I need you on that sack, and I don't care how you get there." Hit by pitch, walk, error, passed ball on the third strike, line drive in the gap, I don't care, but I need you on that sack." Then when he gets there, you need him to wreak havoc.

The best baseball coaching compliment I ever received came in a ball game against our crosstown rival in Arizona. We were hitting and running and stealing and bunting for a base hit and just dumbfounding their defense that day. It was late in the game, maybe the sixth inning, and we had already bunted for a base hit successfully three times. We're up something like 10-1 and we've got runners on first and second and nobody out and our leadoff hitter at the plate, a guy who has already bunted for a base hit once on the day.

Their third baseman is trying to figure out where to play. He's got to defend against a batted ball, so he needs a little depth to give him an angle. Normally in that position he plays even with the bag at double play depth. But he's got to defend the steal of third, too, so he's got to cheat to his right, nearer the bag. And he's got to defend the bunt, too, because that's a "bunt in order" play, so he really needs to come in on the grass. And of course we've already successfully bunted for a base hit several times that day.

The player kinda threw up his hands and asked his coach, "Where do you want me to play?" And the coach says to him from the dugout, in a tone of resignation and defeat, "With these guys, I don't have any idea." That is the confusion and dismay that you hope to inflict on your opponents by your brand of aggressive offensive baseball.

We talked a little earlier about first pitch swinging and your hitters not taking a lot of pitches in high school ball. Let me qualify that. That's true, but in certain spots in the batting order, like the leadoff man, you'll normally want to coach him to be more cautious when he's ahead in the count. Why? Well, if your leadoff guy is indeed an excellent baserunner who can really move, and he's ahead 2-0 in the count on the game's first two pitches, it's wise to have him be very selective on that third pitch. Make the guy on the hill prove he can throw strikes. If a walk gets your leadoff guy on base, that's fine. Whatever gets him there works.

It's been said often, and I think it's especially true in high school baseball, that the most difficult six outs for the pitcher and the defense to record are the first three and the last three. So your leadoff guy is ahead 2-0 or even 3-1 in the game's first at bat, he needs to be very selective. You want him to hit the ball hard and set the tone for your offense; but more than that, you want him on base. Many high school pitchers are a little shaky making their first pitches of the contest. So if you're going to take at all, that's the spot to do it.

Say the pitcher recovers and battles back in the count, makes it 3-2 or 2-2. Now your leadoff guy needs to able to guard the plate with two strikes and needs to be comfortable hitting with two strikes.

Forget The Sacrifice Bunt

Like most coaches, I like a left-handed hitter in the 2-spot, because it's harder for the catcher to throw to second on the steal with a lefty in the box than it is with a right-handed hitter. But as a rule, we don't sacrifice bunt, so we're after a good hitter in the 2-spot, as opposed to a guy who can handle the bat.

If we specialize in small ball, why don't we like the sacrifice bunt? Well, many reasons. But first of all, let's be clear. We don't specialize in small ball, we specialize in speed ball. We can score two or three runs an inning making things happen on the bases, combined with good, solid hitters in the lineup. While we are looking to manufacture runs, we are looking to score more than one run per inning. We're not looking to score one and be done, like many small ball philosophies espouse. We're looking to post a crooked number, we just don't believe in the sacrifice bunt.

They only give you 21 outs in high school baseball. When you sac bunt, you are giving one of those 21 away. That out represents just under 5% of the outs that you are allowed in each 7-inning game. Why give the defense 5% of your outs as a gift? When the opposing team sac bunts and gives us an out, we are thrilled. Now we only have to get 20 more outs that day, or 17 more, if we're ahead after the top of the seventh.

Well, what do you do when you need to advance a runner late in a tie game or tight situation, you may ask? Well, we either swing the bat or we steal or we bunt for a base hit, but we're normally not going to give you an out. A sac bunt is a defensive move, and we want to stay aggressive. One season we stole successfully 43 out of 44 attempts during the heart of the season. If your running game is that good, why give up an out? Just steal the base. Running versus left-handed pitchers? Teach your kids to go on first movement and take your chances. Half the time the pitcher will go home anyway and you've got a great jump. A quarter of the time the pitcher will come to first and the first baseman will catch the pickoff attempt and throw to the shortstop covering second without moving sideways first to procure a good throwing lane, and an errant throw will allow your runner to be safe.

Best left-handed pickoff move in high school I ever coached against belonged to a kid down the road who played for a team outside our district. He stared at a point halfway between home and first, he rolled the knee, he stepped just to the first base side on his move, he did everything the way you teach it, and he was dynamite. Ended up playing four very good years in the SEC. He picked three of our guys off first that day, but only got one of us out. We told our runners that if they got picked, don't try to get back to the bag, just light out for second. The first baseman and shortstop couldn't execute the back end of the play on the other two pickoffs and our runners were safe.

What about the other 25% of the time, you ask? Well, we may get thrown out stealing. But let me ask you. What percentage of the time do you actually sacrifice bunt successfully, especially when the defense knows it's coming?

You see, that's the thing. Sacrifice bunting is much more difficult than it looks. You see sac bunts popped up to the catcher for outs and popped up to the pitcher for outs, all the time. At all levels. Sometimes if the baserunner is edgy and assumes that the hitter will get the bunt down and leaves too soon it turns into a double play. You see players offering at balls out of the strike zone and missing or fouling the ball back. Now your hitter has two strikes on him and what do you do? Do you keep attempting to sac bunt with more pressure on the hitter, who knows he's out if he bunts foul? Or do you say "hit away" with two strikes and the hitter already in a hole in the count?

Even in the bigs you see guys botch the sac bunt, though they get the bunt down successfully much more often than high school kids. But it's not that easy. It has to be practiced daily, with live pitching, and that's difficult on a catcher, so most coaches don't do it. And inevitably, when you want to sac bunt, an RBI guy who hasn't bunted once all year will be at bat. All year you've been telling this player, "Big guy, forget everything else, just relax and swing that stick for us." Now, with the game on the line, you've got to walk down the line to the batter's box and say, "Big guy, I need you to lay one down." Well, shoot, he's out of his comfort zone. He hasn't done it all year, probably hasn't practiced it. They don't teach sac bunting in the crib, it has to be learned daily in practice. And if your no. 5 hitter, a big RBI guy, hasn't been practicing it daily, it's a pretty sure bet that he's not going to suddenly develop good sac bunting skills on the spot?

In addition, the sac bunt puts little pressure on the pitcher and the defense. Sure, they've got to charge in and decide where to go with the ball once it's fielded. But they know in advance, a huge portion of the time, that it's coming. *All bunts work best as a surprise.*

It's the same reason I don't like the squeeze play, as a rule. Now the batter has not only got to get the bunt down, but he's got to bunt the next pitch regardless of where it is, to protect the runner. I say swing the bat, but don't give up an out when you don't have to.

THE 2-SPOT

Whew, all that was in explanation of why we don't need a guy who handles the bat particularly well hitting in the 2-spot! Well, we don't. Again, we prefer a left-handed hitter, hopefully one who can has gap power, a good eye, good speed, and a little patience. A guy with a discerning eye is a good choice here because it gives your rabbit on first base a few pitches to read the guy on the hill and steal second.

Now, we don't tell guys to take pitches because a baserunner may be stealing. That's for the big leagues. Swing the bat. If you hit a line drive and get the baserunner doubled off because he was stealing, that's our bad luck. Start the runner anyway, and let the hitter swing away. Run and hit, baby, not hit and run. Starting the runner will open up holes in the middle infield (on the steal of second) and a guy hitting in the 2-spot who can rip hard ground balls and line drives will give you a lot of first and thirds and you've got to love that.

The Hit and Run

The hit and run? It's tantamount to giving up an out, and normally we don't like it much more than the sac bunt. That's a small exaggeration, but here's what I mean. You've got a runner on first, it's the middle innings, and your no. 2 guy is hitting. The count is 1-0, and the pitcher, who likes to come in with a fastball when he's behind in the count, has proven that he can throw strikes and is around the plate. Good scenario for a hit and run, right?

Well, the cardinal rule for a baserunner on the hit and run is to make sure the pitcher goes home. Because you've got a guy at the plate swinging and protecting you, you don't need the kind of jump that you would ordinarily get on a straight steal. So your baserunner is getting a less than stellar jump. Then your hitter has got to swing the bat, unless the ball is in the dirt, right? That's a common coaching technique on the hit and run. Guy at the plate has got to swing the bat unless the pitcher's offering is way down low. So basically you're telling the hitter, "You've got to swing the bat."

Well, what if the pitch is a hard one to handle, like a fastball up and in and out of the zone. Ever try to get the fat part of the bat on a pitch in that location and hit a hard ground ball through second base? It ain't no picnic. So let's say the hitter swings and misses. Now the catcher has a good shot at throwing out the runner, who has gotten a pedestrian jump.

By calling the hit and run, you've slowed your runner down, you've handicapped your hitter, and you've helped the defense. Just send the runner on a straight steal and have your hitter hit through it if he sees something he likes, and take if he doesn't.

Now, I've seen the hit and run work successfully in high school baseball. You remember our playoff opponent in Georgia that was eating our lunch with little ground balls to the vacated right side of our infield. And in college and pro ball the pitching is so dominant that many times the hit and run is your only option to get something going. And I understand that. But at our level, you've got other things that can advance that runner to second: straight steal, delayed steal, wild pitch, passed ball, error, long sacrifice fly, or a fielder's choice. Or better yet, a base hit. Lot of times you start the runner from first, the batter rips a base hit. And not even a gapper, just a hit that makes an outfielder turn his back to the infield. And you can think about waving the runner all the way home because he was moving on the pitch. It happens.

Now, have we ever called for the sac bunt or the hit and run? Of course. We have it in our arsenal. I occasionally like to call the hit and run with runners on first and second and nobody out against a good pitcher, immediately following an error or a defensive lapse by the opposing team. Oftentimes you'll catch them thinking "we're defending the sac bunt here" and creeping in, which increases your hitting angles. Sometimes you'll catch them on their heels and if your hitter hits a hard ground ball, they may try to turn two and fail because you've started your runners. And sometimes your hitter will swing and miss and their catcher will throw a dart to third and your lead runner will be out, making the first out of the inning at third and violating one of baseball's cardinal rules. It happens, and you've got to be able to live with it if it does. More times than not, though, something good will happen. Put that pedal to the metal and see for yourself.

The Number 3 Hitter

Your no. 3 hitter should be your best hitter. Many times he'll be your best athlete and your best baseball player, and he should be, because he's going to come up in the first inning of every game. This makes it vitally important to put guys in the leadoff and no. 2 spots who can get on base, because you want your no. 3 hitter coming up with runners on base and the pitcher working from a stretch. (Generating baserunners is important if only for the reason that most pitchers don't throw quite as hard from the stretch as from the windup, and most are not as effective from the stretch.)

Avoid asking him to sac bunt, to hit and run, or anything else that will impede his comfort up there. Just tell him, "Swing the stick." If your no. 3 hitter can run, which he frequently can, that's a bonus. Your best RBI guys should hit 3, 4, and 5, with your no. 3 hitter being the most athletic and most capable of stealing a base.

Speaking of an athletic no. 3 hitter, I've got to tell you this story. Funniest, wildest thing that ever happened in all my years of coaching. I'm in my third year coaching in Georgia, and our program is turning the corner. We're not there yet, but we can see the intersection ahead. And we're playing the no. 1 team in the state of Georgia, a team absolutely loaded with talent. They've yet to lose.

We're at our place, and we're facing their ace and we're throwing our best guy. We've battled them in our old run-down ball park, and we enter the bottom half of the seventh tied 5 apiece. Their starter, a tough lefty, is still on the hill, and retires our no. 1 and no. 2 guys. So here's the deal: tie score, two outs in the bottom half of the seventh, nobody on base, and our no. 3 guy at the plate.

Now a word about this kid. Our no. 3 guy was a great, great athlete. Left-handed thrower who could come out of the pen and bring major gas. Played right field and covered it like a blanket and had an absolute hose. Better still, he was a talented left-handed hitter, a tremendous athlete, and a competitor. Had some power, too. Ended up starting four years in the SEC and leading his team to the College World Series his third year. Played a couple of years of pro ball, too. Great kid.

Anyway, it looks like extra innings unless our guy can keep it going here with two outs in the seventh. I mentioned the old ball park with bad lights. Dark as nighttime in Waco, Texas out there in right field. Remember those outfield billboard signs that I had sold prior to the season? Well, they're hanging all over the chain link outfield fence. The billboard signs are thick, and are held onto the chain link with bailing wire, and there's about two inches of space between the chain link and the billboard sign hanging on it.

So their lefty gets behind 2-0 and grooves a fastball. Our kid turns on it and pulls it deep in the alley in right field. Their right fielder turns and sprints back, then slows down. The ball disappears. The field ump has moved out to short right on the play, and as the ball disappears he raises his right hand and forms a circle with his ring finger, signaling home run!

Our kids pour out of the dugout to greet our no. 3 hitter at the plate. We have just unseated an undefeated ball club ranked no. 1 in the state of Georgia, with a solo, walk off homer, with two outs in the bottom of the seventh. We're screaming and celebrating at home plate and our no. 3 hitter is jogging between second and third, lost in his home run trot, when we see a commotion in right field. The right fielder is back at the fence, screaming and holding a baseball. Everybody freezes.

The second baseman sizes up the situation and springs to life in short right field in relay position and calls for the baseball. Suddenly the game is back on! All of us standing around home plate begin yelling at our no. 3 hitter, "Run!" He's no dummy. He senses what's happening, and shifts from a jog to a full speed run. He rounds third and heads home of his own accord, as I'm not there to wave him or stop him. I'm down at home plate with my other players, waiting to shake his hand on the "home run."

Well, our hitter comes barreling down the line. Their catcher, who has already removed his mask, moves to the plate to take the relay throw from the second baseman, and lo and behold, we've got a play at the plate! But there's eighteen kids and three adults (two coaches and the home plate umpire) surrounding home plate and a ton of confusion. Was it a home run? Where did this ball come from? Is this a real play at the plate? What the heck is going on?

The umpire, who has been waiting with us at home plate to make sure that our hitter touched the dish to end the ball game, well . . . he doesn't know what to do. He's as frozen and stunned as we are. But heck, if there's a play at the plate, he needs to call it, so he moves quickly toward the dish.

The ball beats our runner, but short hops their catcher and scoots away behind home plate, where it is lost somewhere among the legs of our players. The confusion and noise is unbelievable. Their catcher scrambles among our players' legs, grabs the ball with his bare hand, and leaps back toward the plate, where our runner is coming in full speed and executes a beautiful hook slide to the infield side of home. The ump signals "Safe!," then yells, "Ball game!," and we all celebrate again!

Well, their right fielder comes racing in, and their coach runs out to the umpire, who is trying to leave the field, and all Hades breaks loose again. What happened was this: Our hitter's "home run ball" cleared the wooden billboard, but didn't go over the top of the chain link fence. Instead, it apparently hit the chain link a couple of inches below the top of the fence, and then got caught between the chain link and the billboard sign. Then, it dribbled down in between the chain link and the billboard, taking a couple of seconds to reach the ground. Which was why their right fielder temporarily gave up on the ball.

Well, the rhubarb lasted for about 10 or 15 minutes. The last thing I remember was the other team's head coach standing in right field, kicking at our billboard sign where the ball had fallen through. And we won 6-5. You've got to love high school baseball.

Middle of the Lineup

Your no. 4 hitter should be able to hit for power, if possible (at the high school level, we work with what we've got), but he's got to be at least good enough to protect your no. 3 hitter. Let's say everybody in the county knows about your no. 3 hitter, who's an all-star. And top of the first, the opposing pitcher retires your first two hitters. Well even in high school ball, a smart pitcher or coach will pitch around a great no. 3 hitter, walk him unintentionally, and take their chances with a mediocre no. 4 hitter.

Going lefty, righty, lefty, righty or righty, lefty, righty, lefty in your lineup is advisable when possible. You send up three left-handed hitters in a row, say they're your no. 4, 5, and 6 hitters, and you run into a dominating left-handed pitcher, one who drops down and has a nasty hook, and you're asking to make three consecutive outs. That's why I like alternating if you can. We don't have a 25-deep bench where we can stack left-handed hitters against a good righty, then have enough right-handed hitting depth to send to the plate when the opposing coach makes a change and brings in a lefty. That's for higher levels. So be careful about hitting guys from the same side in consecutive spots, if you can.

Your no. 5 hitter should be a pure RBI guy, because lots of time he'll come up with runners on (and frequently with two outs, especially in the first inning). You want him to have gap power, and to be a tough, tough out. If you have three guys who have home run power and are capable of hitting for similar averages, hit the most athletic player in the 3-spot, the next most athletic one in the 4-spot, and the least athletic in the 5 hole.

I don't know why, but your no. 6 hitter will lead off a lot of innings. Perhaps it's the math, especially early in the game. First inning, with two on and two outs and no runs in, the game is still defining itself, who is at the plate? Your no. 5 hitter. He either lines one in the alley, or he makes out, but frequently your no. 5 hitter will determine whether the inning is extended or ended. So he needs to be a tenacious hitter and a tough out.

And thus, your no. 6 hitter needs to have leadoff hitter skills, as well as some power, if possible, as we discussed previously. If you have two guys who are excellent candidates to hit leadoff, and one hits better for average and one has a little more power, put the power guy in the 6-spot. Your leadoff hitter will come up at least once a game with nobody on base, so you'll generate more RBI with the power guy in the 6-spot.

You want your no. 6 hitter to be able to bunt for a base hit, to be able to run, and to be able to steal a base. Your leadoff hitter is your Offensive "Igniter." Your no. 6 hitter is your "Reigniter." Sell him on that philosophy. Coach him to understand his role as a second leadoff hitter, especially when he leads off an inning. That's why it's good to have your leadoff hitter and no. 6 hitters reverse roles early in the season and switch spots in the batting order. When your no. 6 hitter leads off an inning, you want him to understand exactly what your leadoff hitter must understand: "You want him on that sack, and you don't care how he gets there."

If there's a spot for a developing player with occasional power, it's the no. 7 spot. The guy hitting in this spot has nothing to think about, just has to go to the plate and hack. And that's good for, say, a sophomore, who is a talented comer but maybe lacks a lot of game experience. He isn't charged with bunting for a base hit, being selective as the leadoff hitter, or anything other than "See the ball, hit the ball."

"Big Dogs"

Work with your no. 3, 4, 5, and 7 hitters together as a group, just as you work with your no. 1, 2, 6, 8, and 9 hitters. Teach your RBI group, or "Big Dogs," to look for pitches they can drive for power. Work with them in the tunnel and on the tee to understand what pitch locations they most like to swing at. Ask them: Where do you like the baseball? What pitch location can you drive for power? They'll know. Coach them in practice when you are "hitting to the count" on 3-1 and 2-0 to look for a pitch in that spot, or something they can really sit on. Coach your "Rabbits," or your 1, 2, 6, 8, and 9 hitters, to be more selective in those situations, since they are so valuable as baserunners.

I like to give my RBI guys a green light on 3-0 unless the pitcher is just all over the place. In fact, they know they've got the green light on 3-0 unless they look down and get the take sign. You see some of the best pitches to hit in high school baseball on 3-0. We've had a lot of success swinging on that count. Have we popped up some? Yes. Have our hitters offered at less than good pitches and bailed the pitcher out of a jam? Sure, occasionally. But the aggressive mindset of hitting 3-0 is worth a lot. Your kids will feel like they've got an advantage that other teams don't have. They'll smile down at you in the box and lick their lips when they look down and don't see the take sign on that count. Try it.

We already talked about the role of the 8 and 9 hitters: Get us back to the leadoff spot in any way you can. Doesn't mean they don't hit for average or power. Doesn't mean they always bunt for a base hit. Just means they are very good at avoiding outs and getting on base. And then doing some damage once they get there.

Last thing about lineups. Get your hitters some at bats, especially early in the year. You want to see how kids compete in actual game conditions as opposed to practice.

I'm in my first year in Arizona, and I think I've got our lineup figured out pretty good. I think I know who can hit and who can't. So I set the lineup in about the fifth game, and I stick with it. All season.

Now, every so often, not enough to bother me, but just to plant a bug in my ear, my backup second baseman says, "Coach, how about letting me take a swing in a game sometime." And I say, "Clint, we'll do it." But in the back of my mind I know I've already got a set lineup that I like.

You know the drill. You only get so many games in a high school season. So you rarely play your backups. That's why you rarely see a backup catcher starting a high school game. The best catcher catches every game. The season is just too short for using all your players.

Well, one day my first baseman has the flu and we're playing on the road. Now the kid who is sick is with us, and he says he can play, but I can see in his eyes that he feels awful. Now here's a perfect spot for Clint to step in and hit. But I can't bring myself to put him in the lineup. I start my sick first baseman and he takes an "O'fer."

This goes on all season long, and Clint never gets off the bench. Then, with three games left in the year, my starting second baseman hurts his knee on a play at the plate. So now I've got to play Clint. Not only do I need his bat in the lineup, but he's our backup second baseman.

So I stick Clint down in the 8-spot. First game out, first time up, he sits on a fastball and rips a double to right. Next time up, base hit up the middle. Next game, two more hits. Third game, same thing. I mean this kid is hitting a ton, and he's got gap power, too. We lose in the finals of our district tournament, but Clint hits in every game.

That taught me something. For at least the first 10 games of the year, let some guys hit. Maybe they'll rise to the occasion and surprise you. If I had done that with Clint, instead of just sticking with the same lineup, I would have discovered his "game" abilities, because truthfully, he never blistered the ball in practice. He was a game-time hitter.

Looking back, I could have played him at first the day my regular had the flu. I could have DH'd him throughout the year. I could have used him as a pinch hitter in certain spots. But I should have gotten his bat in the lineup.

CHAPTER EIGHT
OFFENSIVE SIGNS AND SIGNALS

"Just gimme some kind of sign girl . . .
to show me that you're mine."

Just Gimme' Some Kind of Sign as performed by Brenton Wood

Review your offensive signal package every day. We reviewed ours during stretching exercises.

Your signs should be simple enough for your players to readily understand and execute, but not so transparent that the opposition can easily detect them. Concentrate on communicating non-verbally with your players during stretching or sign sessions. Far more runs are lost from your own team misunderstanding and/or missing signs than from opposing teams detecting your signs and making strategic moves to counteract you.

I practiced many hours in front of a mirror delivering signs. It takes a while to become adroit at delivering signs with both hands, but with practice, anyone can do it.

SELECTING AN INDICATOR

Start with selecting your indicator, which is of course the sign after which your "live" sign is delivered. I always "slowed" my signaling process as I was about to use the indicator and the "live sign" to make sure that our players were on the same page. Sometimes I went to the indicator and the "live" sign immediately afterwards twice in the same sequence. In high school ball, you can do this without much danger of opposing teams stealing your signs and making moves to offset you.

I think you also need a "rub off" sign, which removes any previous sign delivered during the sequence. Some coaches have a "start over" sign, which means "We've miscommunicated, let's start over after this signal." For me, it's either "We're live" or "We're not," because I never wanted to start over while signaling for fear that the hitter and/or runner(s) would be confused. If there was confusion on a sign delivered on say, a 1-0 count, I simply went to the "wipe off" sign, and waited for the next sign sequence after the next pitch to put on a "live" sign. If we absolutely had to have something working on that pitch, we went to the "wipe off" sign, then directly to the indicator and the "live" sign, and we communicated pretty well that way.

Figure 5. Review your signal package every day during stretching exercises. Our indicator was either hand to the bill of the cap. Fist over fist was "bunt for a base hit."

Some coaches use the team nickname across the jersey as an indicator. Let's say your team is the Tigers. If your steal sign is either hand to the cap, the coach would wipe his hand across the "Tigers" lettering on the chest, then touch the cap. By going to the team nickname only when a "live" sign is to follow immediately, the players can easily follow the next sign and attempt to execute it.

I personally like to use the team letters across the chest as a "wipe off," meaning "there's nothing live to be delivered on this pitch." I liked that because the signaling action mimics the meaning of the sign: You are wiping your hand across your chest, and "wiping out the play," to give the "wipe off" sign.

Sometimes, if I wanted to "show" our "live" signs to the opposition, but not use them, I would start the signaling process with the "wipe off," and then go to our steal or squeeze or bunt for a hit sign, and of course nothing would be "live." But I made sure not to confuse our own players. Oftentimes I would start the signaling process by "wiping off" across the chest three times in the first five signals given. For instance, I might give the "wipe off" across the chest with the left hand, go to the cap with the right hand; come back across the chest with the left hand; go to the ear with the right hand; and then come back across the chest with the left hand again.

Our hitters and baserunners knew from the very first sign (wipe off across the chest) that nothing was "live" on this sequence. But since the ear was often our steal sign, and the cap was often our indicator sign, we "showed" the two signs that we used most often (the indicator and the steal) in a "dead" sequence.

Some coaches like to make only one hand "live," and one hand "dead," for giving signs. You can, for instance, make the left hand "live" during odd innings and the right hand "live" during even innings. Let's say your indicator is the chin and your steal is the belt buckle. In the top of the first inning, with a hitter at the plate and a runner aboard, you can go to the chin (your indicator) and the steal (your belt buckle), but use your right hand, and it's a "dead" sign, because it's an odd-numbered inning (the first). So you've showed the opposition your indicator and your steal sign, but they're not "live" because the correct hand wasn't used.

We always told our players that either hand was always "live" for fear they would get confused.

Here is a typical offensive sign package:

Indicator: Either hand to cap and next sign is "live"

The following signs are "live" only following an indicator:

Steal: Either hand to either ear

Delayed Steal: Either hand to either wrist

Steal of Home: Both hands to both ears, one after the other

Bunt for Hit: One fist on top of another

Squeeze: Either hand to opposite shoulder

Hit and Run: Either hand to chin, nose and back to chin

First and Third:

Vs. Lefty Play: Right hand to left elbow, then down the arm to the wrist

First and Second:

Jam Up Play: Either hand to either elbow

The following signs are "live" without an indicator:

Take: Either thumb up (no indicator)

Sacrifice Bunt: Either thumb down (no indicator)

Run on your own: Wipe "up" in three consecutive spots (no indicator)

Don't run: Wipe "down" in three consecutive spots (no indicator)

You might also employ offensive signs for a "fake steal" or "fake bunt and slash hit." We've used both of these plays and had them in our offensive signal package in the past.

Let's talk about the package listed above, starting with signs prefaced by an indicator. For the steal, we just touch the tip of the cap with either hand, then go immediately to either ear with either hand. Most years, it is our most frequently used sign.

You will notice that the squeeze play sign mimics the meaning of the word "squeeze." By grabbing the left shoulder with the right hand, or the right shoulder with the left hand, the third base coach is "squeezing" a part of his body. This action mimics the meaning of the word "squeeze" and helps you communicate the action to your players. Since we use the squeeze play so infrequently, we usually want to utilize a sign that is different, like this one, in addition to one that mimics the word's meaning.

Some years we required our hitter and our runner to acknowledge the squeeze sign by going to the cap with either hand, but I think this gives the defense cause for pause and can create a greater likelihood of them pitching out or trying a pickoff play to offset the squeeze, so we did away with the recognition sign requirement from the player. Almost always on the squeeze or the steal of home, I'd move over closer to the runner on third and get a "eye confirmation" that the runner got the sign. On the squeeze, also, I might say to the runner, "Wait until his stride foot hits," which is code for "Did you get the sign?" and instructional for "Avoid leaving too early and tipping the play." If you say to the runner at third, "Wait until his stride foot hits," and the runner looks at you like you're from Mars, you either call time or get your hitter's attention and give him the "Wipe Off" sign.

You'll also notice that the "hit and run" sign, which is the indicator then the finger to the chin to the nose and back to the chin, mimics the three words in "hit and run." The "hit and run" is our only three-word play, so we made the sign our only three-touch sign. This is a physical reminder to the players what is happening.

The sign for the "First and Third vs. Lefty" play mimics the action of the play, also. We signed by putting the right hand on the left elbow, which reminds our players of the play because we're facing a left-handed pitcher. Then we pulled the right hand down the left arm to finish the sign, which reminds the runner on first to stretch his lead to entice the pickoff throw. The action of "pulling" the hand down the arm reminds the baserunner to "stretch" his lead. Again, the sign chosen mimics the action of the play, making it easier for the players to remember.

Signing Without an Indicator

I don't know how many other ball clubs use some of their signal package without an indicator, but it's a homegrown idea and makes a lot of sense to me. If you're going to give your players a "take" sign, many times it'll be on a 3-0 pitch. And most times the opposition will be looking at you, along with your hitter.

So why give them a look at your indicator sign prior to putting on the "take" sign? Just give the "take" sign by itself, with no other signs and no indicator. The fact that they know your "take" sign isn't much of an advantage to the opposition. Almost everybody takes on a 3-0 count and their pitcher still has to throw a strike.

When you want to put the sacrifice bunt play on, many times it'll be in this situation: nobody out and runners on first and second. Right? Here's another opportunity for your opposition to read your signs and steal your indicator and bunt sign in an obvious bunt situation. So simply skip the indicator, skip other signs, and go directly to your "bunt" sign, and give that and that alone to your hitter and runners. Most times the defense knows it's a bunt situation and has already called a bunt defense, so you're not giving them any information that they don't already have.

Not every coach likes signaling with no indicator, but it never hurt us, and it's an easy message to impart most times.

With our better players, we liked to green-light them during the course of the season. That is, these runners had been told sometime during the season that they can run on their own. Because it involves both the coach and the team trusting the runner's baseball intelligence and instincts, we made it a small ceremony in our clubhouse every time we green-lighted a runner. Then we presented a small green paper lantern to the player, who would hang it in his locker.

Players are people, and they like being told that they can handle a responsibility and that they are trusted. In all the years we green-lighted runners, I've only had to take one paper lantern out of a locker and tell a player that he's lost his green light. Since being given the green light to run is an honor on our team, players who have not been green-lighted will often ask, "Coach, when can I run on my own?"

This is exactly what you want, because now you've got your players thinking about baserunning and about being excellent, honored teammates on the bases. When a player asks if he can run on his own, that's a perfect time to talk baserunning strategy with him. Does he know to play it safe with nobody out? Does he know that we want to try to score him any way we can with two outs? In other words, work with him on his baserunning IQ. Set some mutual goals with him, and tell him you'll watch his progress. To get green-lighted, he's got to reach base first, so he's going to be motivated to work on his hitting, too.

You coach a green-lighted runner differently when he gets on base. Now, in our system, green-lighting a runner did not mean that the runner could take off any time he wanted to. What it meant was this: If the runner gets an "upswipe" sign, he's free to run on any pitch during that at bat. You simply swipe up on your body, anywhere, three times, with no indicator and no other signs, and you are telling your runner: "I think you can steal on this guy and it's a running situation. It's up to you when you go during this at bat."

The runner knows now that you think it's a good steal situation and that he should go when he gets a good jump, or when he thinks the pitcher will deliver an off-speed pitch. He also knows to be aggressive off his secondary lead on any ball that gets away from the catcher.

To deliver the "Run on your own at your own discretion during this at bat," you can swipe "up" on either side of your jersey, up on either leg, up on either arm. Just move your hand "up" in a swiping motion three times, anywhere on your uniform, and deliver no other signs.

Better players like being green-lighted for several reasons. One, they are playing the game in a more professional manner. Everybody on our team knows who's got the green light, so when they steal a base, everybody knows that the chances are the player accomplished something using his own baseball sense, and his teammates admire him for that. That's very satisfying to young athletes. Another advantage is that players sometimes get a poor jump on a pitch, and if they've been told to steal, in most systems they've got to run anyway. This way, if the player gets a great jump, or reads breaking pitch, or sees a ball trickle away from the catcher, he knows he's got the approval to run and he simply makes the decision on his own. But if he gets a poor jump, or isn't confident he can steal the bag, he doesn't have to go.

Now, if you don't want your player to run on the at bat, all you've got to do is swipe "down" on your body three times, using no indicator and no other sign. Here you're telling your runner: "We're not going unless it's a passed ball to the backstop, because it's not a running situation." When might this occur? Well, let's say your leadoff man walks on four pitches and the opposing pitcher has yet to throw a strike. You might consider giving your green-lighted runner three "down" swipes and telling him "don't run now," because the pitcher hasn't proven he can throw the ball over the plate. So let's don't give the defense a break by running and offering them a possible out when they can't throw the ball over the plate.

Certain situations call for the steal, and even with green-lighted runners, you can call for the steal and the runner must run on that particular pitch. So with our system, you've still got the same control of the running game as you did without green-lighting runners, but you've empowered some of the players on your team to "coach themselves and be a more integrated part of your team's running game."

Opposing teams never pitched out when we signaled the green light to a runner by swiping "up" on the uniform three times. They never held the ball, or stepped off, or tried numerous pickoffs, as if they knew we were running on that pitch. Swiping "up" three times with no indicator and no other sign is a hard thing to decipher for the opposition, and since the baserunner may not steal on the pitch immediately following that "up" swiping, the opposition rarely connects the sign with the action of stealing.

If we got first and second, I would usually give three "downswipes" to the lead runner. Here's why. I didn't want him taking off on his own, and the trail runner not knowing when the lead runner is stealing. This can leave the trail runner not getting a good jump, or not going at all. So if we got first and second, I'd usually give the runners a "don't run downswipe," then if we wanted to double steal or put something on, I'd go to the indicator and the steal sign, and both runners knew they had to move on the pitch.

Now, this green-lighting was good for stealing second and third, but not home. No runner had the green light for stealing home. The hitter is involved and safety is an issue, so I made that call. But you have to have it in your sign package. I've seen the steal of home win games in high school. I've seen it disrupt games and ruin the composure of a pitcher.

To do it successfully, you've got to practice it and talk about it with your team. One reason that many high school teams don't steal home more often is the difficulty with signaling both the runner and the hitter simultaneously. Because you've got to have the hitter in on the play. You can't have a right-handed hitter swinging away and causing a potential injury problem. And you've got to have your hitter give the runner access to the plate. That is unless you're going to use the old 50s and 60s semi-pro play, where the hitter holds his ground and the runner is coached to slide right through his outstretched legs. I've never seen this play executed live, but I've had friends tell me they've seen old time teams do it. Whew.

Now, two years ago I'm watching a college baseball game on television. And there's a runner on third with two outs and it's early in the count. The runner gets a great primary lead, and when the pitcher begins his motion, the runner takes off for home on the steal. The hitter holds his ground in the box, and very early on the pitch (the ball is still halfway to the plate), the hitter actually takes a high swing and purposely misses the ball. He's way out in front of it. After his swing is completed, and then and only then, he moves back with his left foot to give the runner room to slide to the plate.

It was obviously a coached play, and designed of course to create as much traffic in front of the catcher as possible as the runner comes barreling in. And it worked like a charm. I'm not sure I would use this play in high school, for a couple of reasons, but it was fascinating to watch. You see just about everything in college baseball if you're attentive and watch enough ball games.

Now, back to signaling two players simultaneously. In the signal package above, the sign for the steal of home was both hands to both ears, one after the other. I waited until I had the attention of both the runner on third and the hitter, and I went to the indicator, the "steal of home sign" (both hands to both ears, one after the other), then I went to our "take" sign, which was "one thumb up." So the hitter sees the sign for the "steal of home," and he sees the sign for "take," and he knows his job. He's coached to stand in like he's awaiting a pitch, hold his ground until the pitch leaves the pitcher's hand, and then move his left foot and body out of the box by turning toward the third base dugout, just as if he's moving his left foot out to take a sign prior to the pitch. With left-handed hitters, they can just hold their ground and of course, leave the bat on their shoulder. But I can't recall ever calling for the steal of home with a lefty hitting. Didn't steal third very often with a lefty hitting, either. If you've got to, you've got to, but odds are more in your favor with a right-handed hitter up there.

Trail runners must see the sign as well, so if you've got a first and third and you call for the steal of home, you've got to communicate your sign to three players simultaneously (two baserunners and a hitter). You don't want to tip the defense off that a play is on, so you've got to sign in your normal fashion, and that means that all three players have to be ready to receive the sign immediately after the previous pitch. Naturally, you want your trail runner to be stealing on the pitch if the lead runner is stealing home. And he needs to be going full speed.

Speaking of trail runners, here's another college game story I saw on television recently. The offense has runners on first and second and they put on the double steal. The runner on second is off with the pitch and the trail runner attempts to take second. But there's a tiny delay before the trail runner takes off, as he waits to make sure the lead runner is going. (That's assuming he got the sign. Maybe he didn't get the sign and just began his move to steal second when he saw the lead runner attempt his steal.) At any rate, the double steal is on, and the lead runner gets a great jump.

I'm waiting for the play at third, but the catcher receives the pitch, comes out of his crouch, and fires the ball to the second baseman covering second. And the runner is out by three feet. It's the second out of the inning. The pitcher gets the next hitter to pop out, and the defense stymies a big inning by the opposition and wins the game.

Why mention this? It's about the importance of communication, both on offense and defense. Had the trail runner picked up the double steal sign successfully, and been off with the pitch and trusted that the lead runner had also picked up the sign, he would have a much better chance of stealing second. Since the lead runner had third stolen cleanly, the team would have had second and third with one out, and would have an excellent chance to post a crooked number and win the ball game.

Now, defensively, how did the catcher know to attempt to throw out the trail runner? Furthermore, how did the middle infielder know to cover the bag? Well, it's successful communication with more than one player simultaneously, on the defensive side.

You've got to coach your hitters to step out immediately after each pitch. And you've got to coach your baserunners to "bust it back to the bag" after every pitch, and then look for their sign at once. If you have to whistle and gesture and make an effort to gain the attention of your hitters and baserunners in order to put a play on, you're usually better off not signing to them. It may or may not get through and the defense goes on "high alert."

Another advantage of having everybody looking at you immediately after each pitch is that you may want to simply "swipe down" to your runner, meaning "don't run in this at bat," and clap your hands to your hitter, meaning "there's nothing on and hit your pitch, big guy." Then your baserunner and your hitter can relax and play baseball. Either way, you've got to establish immediate and effective non-verbal communication with your hitters and baserunners to maximize your team's offensive potential. This is the reason we sprint to first on a walk. We want everybody's attention as quickly as possible after the previous pitch. Then we want to sign and receive, and play good baseball.

Non-Signal Hand Gestures and Yells

There are several hand gestures and yells that we commonly used that were not an official part of our offensive sign package, but that were just as effective and vital as the steal and bunt for a hit signs. Here are a few that you might consider using:

Hand Gestures

Hands form a small rectangular box in front your stomach.	This pitcher is struggling throwing strikes; make him throw it right into the little box that I'm forming with my hands. Avoid helping him by swinging at a bad pitch.
Hands palms down at eye level, moving back and forth.	A message to your baserunner(s) to make a line drive go through; avoid getting doubled off.
Waving (windmilling) with either arm.	Round the bag and keep running.
Pointing to the next base.	Same message; keep running.
Both hands palms down, pressing downward.	It's a close play; slide.
Pointing downward toward the base.	Keep coming hard, but the ball is nearby, so stop right on the bag.

Verbal Signals

"On the bag, on the bag."	Keep coming hard, but the ball is nearby, so stop right on the bag.
"Round it, round it."	Keep coming hard, and round the bag and find the ball.
"Be alive on a ball in the dirt."	Focus on your secondary lead and be prepared to advance on a ball that's not handled cleanly
"That's good right there."	Retreat to the bag you've rounded, after advancing on a passed ball
"Come hard."	Usually given to runner coming to third; means we may be able to take home
"Nobody out . . . Play it safe."	Message to runners to avoid taking chances now because we're likely to score them later in the inning
"Going on downward contact now."	Telling runner at third base to sprint for home on any ground ball.
"Make it go through."	Telling runner at third base to hold his ground and wait to sprint for home until ball clears the infield.

These are just a few of the hand gestures and verbal cues that we used to communicate with players during a game. A great offensive team is watching the game, digesting it, and reacting with constant communicative efforts.

You will remember early in the book I told the story of our leadoff hitter who stole home successfully when he thought the squeeze play was on? And I said concerning that event "That a nod's as good as a wink to a blind mule?" Well, it's true. It's not how good your signal package is, or how sophisticated a method you develop of delivering your signs. What matters is how effectively you communicate. How well do your players get your message?

My last year in Texas I coached a wonderful player named Stan. Guy could play infield or outfield, could catch or pitch, could hit leadoff and get on base, could hit third and drive in runs. Just a great all-around player. Had exceptional athletic skills. I used to call him "The Dancer" because when he turned the double play from his position at shortstop, he would sprint to the bag, receive the toss and make the play at second, then throw to first and execute the most professional-looking pirouette you ever witnessed. He was absolutely great at "busting it around the bag" at second, making the throw to first, then "dancing" out of the runner's way. He was just so athletic, it was a thrill watching him compete. Most of his skills came naturally to him and I didn't coach him on his defensive technique very extensively. Didn't need to.

He had a learning disability, though, and was the only player on our team who had difficulty deciphering and executing offensive signs and plays. Sometimes he ran when got the "steal" sign, but sometimes he didn't. You just never knew if he got the sign or not.

After a month or so of the spring high school season, I called him over to the side during practice, and told him in confidence, "Stan, you're a great athlete. And I'm gonna' turn you loose, at the plate and on the bases. You and I are gonna' have a special signal package, and it's all going to be verbal and pointing, no signs. If I want you to steal, I'm simply going to point to the next base. If I want you to stay put and not run, I'm just gonna' shake my head sideways and that means, "No, don't run." If I want you to bunt, I'm going to pretend that I'm bunting as if I have a bat in my hands. If I want you to take, I'm just going to shake my head "No," as in, "Don't swing. Now you're the only player that I'm doing this for."

I never alluded to his disability, or to the fact that he wasn't picking up our signs. We just figured out a way to get him to do what we wanted him to do, a way to communicate. And truthfully, no opposing teams ever gained an advantage on us because of the obvious signs I was giving him. You do what you have to do to communicate. It's not how much you know, it's how much your players understand that counts.

CHAPTER NINE
BUNTING FOR A BASE HIT

"As I was motivatin' over the hill . . . I saw
Maybelline in a Coup De Ville . . .
A Cadillac a'rollin' on the open road . . . but nothin' outruns
my V-8 Ford."

Maybelline as performed by Chuck Berry

The bunt for a base hit was such a vital component of our offensive repertoire that it deserves its own chapter.

For you, it may not be such a frequently-utilized weapon in your arsenal. But it seemed wherever I landed in coaching, all the big home run hitters had just graduated, and what I had to work with were players of smaller stature.

That's not all bad, but small and weak and slow is a bad combination. You've got to get strong in your off-season weight training program. And you've got to find speed somewhere in the hallways of your school, and recruit it from other sports in your school, and emphasize it daily to your team. CONSTANTLY EMPHASIZE THE IMPORTANCE OF SPEED. Work on getting faster and running the bases and getting on base.

A team with several players who can run and who can hit for average with occasional gap power, and who can bunt successfully for a base hit, has a great advantage over a similar team whose players cannot bunt for a base hit. You'd still rather have four or five mashers, but in lieu of that, you emphasize and develop and incorporate speed into your program because you must.

It's like this. If a kid can walk and chew gum, and he's left-handed, we're going to put him on the mound and see if we can't teach him to throw strikes. Likewise, if a kid can really run, we're going to teach him how to bunt for a base hit, and then how to wreak havoc on the bases. And we're going to try to make a hitter out of him. And make him a tough out. You work with the weapons you've got.

I cannot emphasize how important this is in maximizing your offensive potential in high school baseball. The ability to coach this skill, and implement it successfully, can be the difference in winning six or seven ball games a year that you might have lost.

Let's say you play in a very competitive league, which many of you do, where the starting pitching is excellent and even if you're facing a team's no. 2 or no. 3 starter, you're seeing a guy with good stuff. How many base hits per game do you average against this kind of pitching? Let's say six or seven, just for our purposes here. In a 3-2 ball game, which is well-pitched, it's not unusual for a team to garner only six base hits. Let's say the opposing pitchers walk two of your players and that one of your players reaches on an error, in addition to these six hits. So you've generated a total of nine baserunners. And let's say you were the home team, and you used all 21 of your outs. Add these 3 numbers (6 hits, 2 walks, and an error) together, and we can see that you forced the opposition to face 30 total hitters (unless they turned a double play, and we'll assume that they didn't).

Okay, so let's do the math. You're getting 9 baserunners aboard out of every 30 at bats, which translates to the fact that about 30% of your hitters are getting on base. Now, let's say you bunted for a base hit successfully, just twice, in this same contest. And let's say that the guys who bunted successfully for a base hit did not do so at the expense of getting a base hit.

In other words, had they not bunted for a hit, we'll assume they would have made out. This is not always the case, but outs are what we have most of in baseball, so let's go with it. That increases your total number of baserunners to 11, out of those same 30 at bats, and also means that now about 37% of your hitters are reaching base. These 11 baserunners represent more than a 22% increase in the number of your hitters that reach base.

These numbers do not take into account the disruption of the defense, and the extra bases taken and extra runs scored, by adding these two bunts for a hit each game. Quantifying how many more bases were taken, and how many more runs were scored, is difficult, especially when you factor in the tendency of high school defenses to make errant throws on surprise bunt attempts. But suffice it to say, after coaching high school baseball for 20 years, if anything, I think this mathematical analysis undervalues what bunting for a hit brings to your team.

Let's talk about why bunting for a hit can be such a valuable part of your offensive arsenal.

- It may be the only way that player can reach base that day. Many times the pitching we encountered was so overpowering that a player's chances of reaching base were much greater on the bunt for a hit than on swinging the bat.

- The threat of players bunting for a hit forces the cornermen to play closer to home plate, opening up better hitting angles when your players swing the bat. It also forces the middle infielders to cheat toward their coverage positions, which can get them moving the wrong way on ground balls and force them into mistakes on routine plays.

- Throwing runners out, especially guys who can really run, on well-placed bunts for a hit is no easy task. We practiced defensing the "slow roller" every day, but most teams don't. Watch how many times high school infielders botch the slow roller or well-placed bunt.

- The well placed bunt is like the offensive answer to the change of pace used by the pitcher. Infielders see hard ground balls and liners and bouncing balls coming at them every day and all game. So when a soft, well placed bunt is laid down in front of them, it is a different kind of play from what they normally make.

Figure 6. The "bunt for a base hit," and all bunts, work best as a surprise weapon. This fielding and subsequent throwing angle demonstrates the difficulty that accompanies this play for a third baseman. My guess is we have a runner aboard here. A sidearm throw on the run that tails into the dirt up the line may put our baserunner at second base.

- It also forces the infielder to throw from a different angle to the bases than he is used to throwing from. A shortstop or third baseman makes

90% of his throws to first and second from a relatively small area of the field, depending on his range. He is used to the throwing angle from that area. On a well-placed bunt, suddenly he is forced to throw to a base from a spot on the field that he does not normally throw from. Sometimes the third baseman and the shortstop must throw visually "through the runner" racing to first, even if the runner is running in the runner's lane.

- Since the ball is not "hit sharply" on a bunt for a base hit, and softly rolls toward the infielder, there is more pressure on the infielder from the crowd and from teammates to make the play. It looks easy. The ball is rolling gently or may even have stopped. It looks like anybody could make the play. So if the infielder botches it, it demoralizes the defense. They appear to have erred on a simple play.

- Lastly and perhaps most importantly, the well placed bunt for a base hit, when properly timed, catches the infield on its heels. *The bunt for a base hit, like all bunts, works best as a surprise.*

Choosing Your Spot: The Long Throw from Third

Many coaches favor bunting toward the right side of the infield. The batter bunts/pushes the ball, or if he's a lefty, drags the ball, just past the pitcher, and to the left of the first baseman. Hopefully, the batter kills the ball just past the pitcher and makes the second baseman come in and make the play.

The good thing about the bunt for a base hit to this side of the infield is that the hitter need only look at where the second baseman is playing. If the first baseman is playing shallow, it's actually to his advantage, because the hitter wants to push the ball by him anyway. If the first baseman is playing deeper, he may or not be able to make the play, but if he does, he's got to throw to the pitcher covering first, and that complicates the play for the defense. If the pitcher fields the ball, the batter has placed the bunt poorly. So you definitely want to push the ball past the pitcher.

The drag bunt was popularized in the 50s and 60s, partly by Mickey Mantle, who was a switch hitter. Mantle would sometimes battle a hitting slump by drag bunting against right-handed pitchers. Hitting from the left side, he would start his movement toward first base and "carry" the ball with him as he manipulated his bat. Mantle's speed was such that usually any bunt that he pushed past the pitcher was good for a base hit. Infielders were usually playing him deep anyway, mostly out of self-preservation. Who wants to try to field a wicked line drive off the bat of Mickey Mantle from close in? Even Ted Williams occasionally bunted for a base hit, because defenses (inspired by Cleveland's Lou Boudreau) had begun shifting toward right field against him. The third baseman wound up playing closer to where the shortstop normally played, leaving a large, unguarded piece of real estate to the right of third base, for Williams to lay down his bunt.

I studied the bunt for a base hit as it is attempted and utilized in high school baseball for many years, and came to the conclusion that we were better off having our hitters attempt to bunt for a hit by bunting the baseball toward third base, rather than toward first base. This was true even for left-handed hitters. There are several reasons for this.

One, the bunt to the right side of the infield brings four potential defenders into the play: the catcher, the pitcher, the first baseman and the second baseman. You will see all four of these players make the play on a bunt to that side. On the bunt to the third base side of the infield, you are normally only dealing with the pitcher, the catcher and the third baseman, so the math is on your side. There's one fewer defender available to make a play.

Now, what about the catcher on the bunt to the third base side? Well, we tried to take the catcher out of the play by bunting the ball hard enough so that even if the catcher fielded the ball, he faced the arduous task of "scooping" the ball into his mitt while he was running toward third base, then turning and making a relatively long throw back toward first base. It's harder than it looks, and while it can be done, you don't want your catcher making that play for a living. So now you basically have the pitcher and the third baseman to deal with.

We always wanted to pressure the third baseman with our bunt for a base hit. Ideally, we want him to have to make a decision and ultimately field the ball. That leaves third base uncovered, which he is loathe to do. If the first baseman charges a bunt and fields it, he knows the pitcher will be covering his bag. As soon as a hitter squares to bunt, the second baseman is taught to move toward first, in case he has to cover the bag, so the shortstop has to move to cover second base. So the shortstop is not really a reliable candidate to cover third base on a bunted ball. With runners aboard, making the third baseman make a decision complicates things for the defense.

Say there's nobody aboard. The third baseman is taught to play well back of the bag, and perhaps to guard the line, depending on the score and the inning. But he is rarely playing even with the bag and hardly ever in on the grass. Because he is taught to play deeper with no runners on, to provide him a wider angle against ground balls, he has given your hitter a large area to bunt to. If the hitter gets the bunt down in the direction of the third baseman, and gets it past the pitcher, he's got a great chance for a bunt base hit. When he gets it down, the pitcher will come off the mound hard, but the ball will roll by him. Then the third baseman will come charging in and be forced to make a Brooks Robinson or Clete Boyer type of skill play, where he barehands the ball and catches it on his left foot and takes one step and throws it on the run off his right foot. This is no easy play.

Now, say there's a runner at first and your hitter lays down a surprise bunt for a base hit. The third baseman, with a runner at first, is usually taught to play at what is called "double play depth," or even with the bag. This cuts down his wider fielding angle from his previous deeper position (with nobody aboard), but it allows him to field a ground ball more quickly and be in a direct throwing line to second base to start the 5-4-3 double play. But it's not a batted ball coming toward him. Instead, it's a rolling bunt. Well, if it's past the pitcher, he's only got one play, and that's to charge the ball and go to first with it.

It's still a tough play for him, even from starting even with the third base bag. The thing is, he may or may not get the out at first, but a vast majority of teams will leave third base uncovered in this situation. Your runner at first keeps flying around second and can take third 95% of the time in high school ball. Traditional defensive thinking is that the catcher should cover third and the pitcher should head toward home plate, but most high schools teams simply don't practice this play. They never see it and don't have the need to work on it very often. Again, your shortstop is going to move to cover second, and your second baseman is going to move toward first, because it's a bunt. There's nobody at third base.

Can your third baseman come charging in and make a difficult play on the run to nip the batter/runner at first, then hustle back to third and take a cross-infield throw from your first baseman, who is normally the weakest throwing and most seldom-used arm in the infield? If the runner at first is getting a good secondary lead when the pitcher delivers and advancing strongly when he sees the hitter square to bunt, he's usually halfway to second base before the bunt hits the ground. There's really no way to stop him from taking third on the play, unless the catcher is coached to cover. Occasionally in high school ball a quick-thinking pitcher, already moving in that direction to make a fielding attempt on the bunt, may continue running and try to cover third. It works sometimes, but the defense has still got to execute a bang-bang play at first on the batter/runner and then the first baseman has still got to throw the ball all the way across the infield, on time and on target, sometimes to a player who is still moving to get there. The odds are certainly in your favor. If the play is executed with nobody out, at the best, you've got first and third and nobody out. At the worst, you've usually got a runner at third and one out.

Now, say you've got a runner at second and nobody out and your hitter lays down a bunt for a base hit toward third base. The defense does not want to allow the lead runner to take third, so this will cause hesitation to charge the ball on the part of the third baseman, who will want to stay home and cover third and hope the pitcher can make the play. But as the play unfolds, and the pitcher and the third baseman see that the pitcher cannot make the play because the ball is intentionally bunted past him, the third baseman will leave his position and charge the ball. Oftentimes it's too late to make a play on the runner at first. More often, you'll see both the pitcher and the third baseman take about three tentative steps toward the baseball, waiting for the other player to make the play, the third baseman will leave third uncovered, and neither player will field the ball and both runners are safe. Now you've got first and third and nobody out. Not only is it a rally builder, it's a defensive demoralizer.

If the third baseman does come in hard and attempt to make a play, in most cases you're shouting at your runner "Come hard! Round it! Round it!," meaning "Round the bag hard at third because I may wave you home." Depending on the difficulty of the angle of the throw and the likelihood of a ball thrown awry toward first, you've got a better than average chance to score that runner if he's coming hard from the get-go, which he's got to do. That's the key. Your runner has got to go full speed off his secondary lead as soon as he sees that the hitter has bunted the ball downward.

The third baseman, knowing you're an aggressive offensive team, has to think about this runner pounding down the line behind him as he makes the play on the rolling or stopped bunt and prepares to throw to first. He knows if his throw is in the dirt or pulls the first baseman off the bag in any way, that there's a good chance that the runner may attempt to score. So in some cases he'll simply hold the ball, wanting to avoid giving up a run on a poor throw. So now you've first and third and something building.

Hitters should bunt the ball to the third baseman and force him to make a decision. Baserunners should transition from an extended secondary lead to a powerful "push off and go" as soon as they see the downward angle of the ball coming off the bat. Pressure the defense in any and every way you can. Pressure, pressure, pressure. Keep up that scare!

You can call for the bunt for a base hit in a myriad of situations, including the ones mentioned above. You can call for it with nobody on and nobody out to start the inning. You can call for it with a runner on third and less than two out. Nothing wrong with calling for it with a runner on third and two outs, but the defense has the advantage then of knowing that if they can get that runner at first, the inning is over. But if that's the only way you can get that runner home, it's better to call for the bunt for a hit, even with two outs, than to stand there and watch your hitter make the third out of the inning with no attempt to score having been made. It depends upon the quality of the pitching you're facing, and the quality of at bats that your hitters are giving you. Get that runner home somehow. You do enjoy the element of surprise in this situation, because few defenses expect you to bunt with two outs.

At what point in the at bat and on which pitch count you call for the bunt for a base hit depends upon a couple of things. First, it's generally easier to bunt the ball successfully against a pitcher who keeps his stuff down in the strike zone. Trying to bunt against guys who throw a lot of high, hard stuff hoping to get a lot of swings and misses upstairs can be troublesome. Bunting the breaking ball can be done, but it's not optimum.

So you want to call for the bunt for a hit against a pitcher who keeps the ball down. You also want to call for it against a pitcher who is predictable when he gets behind in the count. If he misses with a breaking pitch for ball one, is the 1-0 pitch always a fastball? If so, that's the count to call for the bunt for a base hit.

If the pitcher has a tendency to start hitters off with a fastball, then you may want to call for the bunt for a base hit on the first pitch of the at bat.

Normally, you want to give the hitter the sign for bunt for a base hit when the hitter has no strikes. If the hitter already has one strike, and bunts the ball foul, now he's in the hole with two strikes. And of course if you give him the bunt for a hit with two strikes and he bunts foul, then he's out. So it's best to put the bunt for a hit play on when the hitter has no strikes. The 0-0 and 1-0 counts are probably your best choices. If the pitcher gets to 2-0 on your hitter, you may want to turn him loose to swing the bat, hoping the pitcher will groove a fastball, or consider giving him the "take," if the pitcher is really, really struggling.

THE DAILY BUNTING GAME

Your number 1, 2, 6, 8, and 9 hitters should work on bunting for a base hit every day. Your rabbits, the guys who set the table at the top of the order, and the ones at the bottom of the order that get you back to the top of the order, must work on bunting for a base hit every day.

Work the players, the rabbits and their backups, in groups of three, with one player bunting and two players fielding. Visit a marine supply store and buy three 100-feet lengths of thin boat rope (the kind used to tie small boats to a dock). Cut the rope into two 75-foot sections and one 50-foot section. Put the bunter against the backstop behind home plate, then lay down two sets of rope. One piece of rope will extend out from the bunter's front foot and mimic the third base line. Lay down the other piece of rope so that it extends from the bunter's front foot through an imaginary line halfway between the third baseline and the pitcher's mound. The two pieces of rope will look like a triangle with an open end. Now lay down your third section of rope just past the imaginary pitcher's mound (about 60 feet from home plate) that connects the two pieces have already have on the ground. Now your rope really does resemble a triangle. Finally, set 4 or 5 plastic or rubber cones up another 15 feet beyond your cross section of rope. The cones will connect the loose ends of the rope.

Have your players play hard pepper. But instead of hitting the ball, the batter bunts the ball downward and to the left side of your imaginary infield. If the hitter bunts the ball left of the hose representing the foul line, that's a foul ball and he gets no points. If he bunts it right of the hose that represents the halfway point between the foul line and the pitcher's mound, he gets no points there either, because the ball is too close to the pitcher and too easily fielded. If the hitter bunts the ball and it stops somewhere in the triangle, give him one point. If the hitter successfully bunts the ball past the pitcher (beyond the cross rope) and kills it before it reaches the cones, give him three points.

Allow each bunter to attempt six bunts. He doesn't have to offer at every pitch, just as in a real game. But he wants to jump pivot on each throw and prepare to bunt for a base hit, even if he doesn't offer at it.

How To Bunt for a Hit

If you've got a guy who can do it his way successfully, avoid changing his style. But the vast majority of your players will need instruction. Some will think they know how to do it, having tried it occasionally, but many times in game conditions they will foul the ball off repeatedly or bunt the ball too hard in the wrong direction.

Coaching the bunt for a hit is just like coaching hitting: It takes work and time, and you've got to practice it every day.

The first step in teaching the bunt for a hit is the jump pivot. As the pitcher is releasing the ball, and not before, the hitter should simply jump pivot onto the balls of his feet, ending in an athletic position in what would be a slightly closed stance for a hitter. It's not that much of a shift in foot position from the hitter's previous natural batting stance, but it's important that each hitter be taught to forego his normal stance and jump pivot into bunting position. The hitter's bunt position should also include a slight crouch, or bend in the knees. Coaches in many sports like to call this simply an "athletic position," like a basketball player guarding another player. Knees bent, head and back erect, using the balls of the feet.

Have your hitters perform this move, jump pivoting from their natural batting stance to a slightly closed stance, without a bat in hand. Face your hitters, take a windup, and then release an imaginary pitch. The hitters should wait until you reach your release point, then perform their jump pivot.

Now, teach your players to "throw the bat head down." It's a simple movement: The player "throws," or drops the head of the bat down in line with his front foot, while sliding his right hand halfway down the bat. The player's right thumb should be showing above the bat, and his four other fingers should cradle the bat underneath it. The fingers are protected by the bat, should a ball strike that exact spot. But the player's goal is to use the fatter part of the bat beyond his right hand to bunt the ball.

Again, it's a simple movement. Have your players stand in their normal batting stance, then on command, have them drop the head of the bat into bunting position, with the bat being even with the front leg. This will seem awkward to them without the jump pivot, but it's done for a reason. Make sure the players are not only dropping the head of the bat correctly, but moving the hands to get the bat out in front of the plate and even with the front leg.

Now combine your drills. Have your players assume their batting stance, and go through your windup. When you reach your release point, have your players jump pivot and simultaneously drop the head of the bat out in front of the plate, even with the front leg.

The bat should be leveled in front of the imaginary plate at the top of the player's strike zone. I cannot emphasize this enough. After the players have jump pivoted and dropped the head of the bat into bunting position, have them hold their bat in that spot for inspection. Walk around and check the player's feet (weight on the balls of their feet, stance slightly closed), check the position of the hands (left hand in normal hitting position near the knob, right hand about 40% of the way down the bat, with the bat cradled between the thumb and the other four fingers); and finally, *check to make sure the bat is level, in front of the imaginary home plate, and at the top of the player's strike zone.* The bathead should also be held absolutely parallel to the ground. No angling.

Use this practice drill. After your players have jumped pivoted and dropped the bat head, have them lower the bat to meet a ball thrown by you and other coaches and have them bunt the ball directly back to you. Work with them on lowering the entire bat in a level position, using both hands and the knees as an elevator, without dropping either end of the bat. Or without, as we like to say, "angling" the bat. In other words, the player uses both hands to move the bat and up down and bunt the ball.

Actually, he only moves the bat down, and not up, because you want to teach him to avoid offering at any pitch that is above his bat. Why? Well, if he has leveled his bat at the top of the strike zone, and the pitch is above the bat, that pitch is a ball. And two, it's going to be extremely difficult to effectively bunt a pitch that is above the bat.

So throw pitches to your players from about 15 feet away. Use your windup, and have the player jump pivot and drop the head of the bat, leveling it at the top of his strike zone, just as you release the ball. You can stop just before you release the ball occasionally to make sure he is not "tipping" the bunt. But start by having him bunt the ball back to you, and letting a high pitch over the bat pass by.

Then practice with him on "maneuvering the bat" on a level plane in order to bunt the ball toward an imaginary third baseman. It is natural for the player to want to change the angle of the bat and the bat head as he attempts this, but he must be taught to work the bat on a level plane. To do this, he simply moves the bat head toward you, and moves the handle of the bat toward him, as he moves the whole bat down to meet the pitch.

If the bat does not remain level, players will foul pitches off repeatedly. Also, if the ball is not bunted out in front of the plate, many times the ball will come downward off the bat and not be in fair territory. So the player has got to level the bat, and maneuver it in a level fashion, and he's got to get it out in front of the plate, even with his front leg.

Now, add one more component to the drill. Have the player bunt toward third base against your throws, following the same steps in the previous drills, but have him begin his sprint toward first after he sees the ball on the ground. This is probably the one area more than any other where young bunters hurt their chances. They are in such a hurry to scramble toward first that they "overrun" the bunt or before they see the ball and place it properly. Coach your players in the drill not to start their movement toward first until they actually see the ball on the ground, after they have bunted it.

Convince them that a well-placed bunt is much more important than a quick start to first, which it absolutely is. Now, once a player has become accomplished at bunting for a hit against live pitching in a game, he will not actually wait to see the ball on the ground before starting his sprint toward first. But you will notice that he is concentrating longer on seeing the ball and bunting it successfully as he starts to run. And that's what you want.

As far as bunting itself, some have described the process as "catching" the ball, with the hitter providing a little "backwards give" as the ball hits the bat. I think this is a good description of what bunting feels like, but is more apt for sacrifice bunting. We are trying to move the ball past the pitcher, so there's more of a forward action with our bunting attempts. As the players get more comfortable with the bunting game, they will begin to get a good feel for how much "push" should be applied to the ball to bunt it effectively.

Once he can repeatedly bunt successfully following these coaching points, then turn him loose on the bunting/pepper game. Choose an appropriate reward to give to the winner of the bunting game each day, whether it's skipping "equipment" pick up at the end of practice or some other type of incentive.

The best leadoff hitter I ever coached was a wrecking ball named Josh. He was about 5' 8," maybe 165, and a tremendous athlete. He was signed as a running back to play at a Division I school in South Carolina. But during baseball season, he was our centerfielder and our leadoff hitter.

This kid listened to everything I ever told the team about base stealing, bunting for a base hit, primary and secondary leads, stealing third, stealing home—he had it all down. And if you dropped the baseball, or hesitated for a second, or didn't make a quick and accurate play on him at all times, he was just flat out gone. Man, this kid could run, and he had wonderful, aggressive instincts.

We're undefeated in league play one year, and so is our opponent on that day. Well, Josh hits leadoff for us, and he doubles to start the game and then steals third on the next pitch. Comes home one out later on a ground ball to put us up 1-0. Next time up, we've got a runner on third and Josh draws a walk. But he sprints to first, as he's been coached, and makes the turn because nobody's holding him there. And he sees that both middle infielders are standing a long ways from second, and he glances in at the catcher whose still got the ball and is fiddling with his shin guards, and whoosh, he's gone to second. Takes it standing up. They don't even make a throw. We get a base hit and he scores again.

Third time up he singles, steals second, steals third, and comes home on a passed ball. Fourth time up he singles, steals second, steals third, and comes home on a sacrifice fly. We win 6-1, and Josh scored four of our six runs. Don't know how many total bases he accounted for that day, but he just took over the game.

A great leadoff hitter with that kind of aggressive mentality can turn the tide in your favor in an otherwise close ball game. Truth be told, without him, we probably don't win that day, or it would have been a heckuva' lot closer game. The point is, Josh was green-lighted from day 1, and coached to play aggressive offensive baseball. He was never thrown out that day while trying to advance, but if he had been, we would have lived with it and encouraged him to keep running, to keep heading for home.

Josh was on the road to South Carolina in August of his freshman year for his first days at college and with the football program when he was hit head-on by a car that veered into his lane for no apparent reason. Both Josh and the other driver were going a good 65-70 mph on a 2-lane road. Josh almost died. He survived, underwent several surgeries, and had metal rods put in his legs. Never played another down or inning of organized athletics.

CHAPTER TEN
COACHING BASERUNNING

*"People say believe half of what you see . . .
And none of what you hear."*

I Heard It Through the Grapevine **as performed** by Marvin Gaye

During tryouts my second year as a head coach I announced that we were going to time all the players going home to third. A young man whom I didn't know jumped to the start of the line. He had not played in our summer program, in fall ball, or with our high school program, but he was obviously eager, and thought that foot speed was one of his attributes, so he moved into position to be the first player timed.

The youngster took his batting stance and prepared to take his natural swing, as directed, before running against the stopwatch. I shouted the verbal command "Go," and he swung the bat at an imaginary pitch and dropped it, turned to the left, and sprinted directly from home to third base.

Well, our returning players and the rest of the kids at the tryout got a jolt out of that, because obviously, the drill was organized to time players going from home to third in a ninety-yard sprint, not a thirty-yard dash. But the thing is, the young man did exactly what I told him to, which was run from home to third. I did not specify that we were going to touch first and second along the way or anything else. I just said, "Swing the bat with your natural swing, drop the bat and run home to third."

My first year coaching in Georgia, as I have mentioned, I took over a program that was in tatters. I was just beginning to get to know the returning players, evaluate their abilities and install our system. And about our third game of the year, we were playing a team whose pitcher was struggling throwing strikes.

He had thrown seven balls in a row and was on the verge of walking our no. 8 hitter on four pitches. So I called over our no. 9 hitter on deck and I said, "Kevin, if he walks Ronnie here on four pitches, I want you to take the first pitch." Kevin looked at me and nodded that he understood.

Well, Ronnie indeed walked on four pitches. Now we have first and second, nobody out, and the pitcher has thrown eight straight balls. Kevin stands in, gets comfortable, and the pitcher delivers. It's about shoulder level or higher, well up and out of the strike zone. And Kevin lets loose with a huge swing and miss that surprises everyone in the ballpark. Didn't come close to hitting the baseball, and the pitcher catches the return throw from the catcher in grateful shock that we have given him a gift when he was struggling so badly with his control.

I was really miffed. After all, I had just told Kevin to take the first pitch. So I call time and meet Kevin halfway down the third base line. "What are you doing?" I say. "Didn't I tell you to take the first pitch?"

Kevin stares right at me, and as big as Dallas, says, "Coach, I did. I took it and swung at it as hard as I could." I kid you not.

Was Kevin to blame? No, not really. It was poor coaching. I was so new to the program and had spent so little time installing our system with the kids that one of our players truly did not understand that when I said 'Take,' I meant "Leave the bat on your shoulder."

Veteran baseball men will have a hard time imagining either of these scenarios. I can hardly believe that this happened myself, as I look back on it now. But it did. So it's important to remember, we're dealing with 16-year-old kids here.

What you say and what they hear, or what you are trying to communicate and what they understand, may be two completely different things.

One last, true story, and it's a recollection of a baserunning incident that will resonate with you as a coach. Okay. We're playing for the district championship on the road. We've already swept this opponent in regular league play; now we've got to beat them at their place in the district tournament championship.

They get three runs on us in the top half of the first. But we settle down and start our comeback. By the fourth inning, we've taken the lead and we're ripping line drives and taking extra bases and assuming command of the game. We're leading 5-3, have runners on first and second with one out, and we're about to tear the game wide open. Our no. 9 hitter, who is leading us in hitting, rips a shot into the right field alley.

Our lead runner at second freezes momentarily, makes the ball go through, and then heads full steam toward me at third. I wave him home and forget about him and then turn my attention to the trail runner. The ball is behind the trail runner, in right field, so he's looking to me just before he gets to second base to see if he should attempt to take third, just as he's supposed to do. Their right fielder, meanwhile, has raced over into the alley and made an excellent play on the ball, and a good throw from him in right will nail our trail runner at third base, so I hold up my hands in the "Stop" sign position, and yell, "That's good right there!," which means that the trail runner should stop at second base. Well, he does, so everything is good, right? We now lead 6-3, we've got a runner on second with one out, and our leadoff hitter at the plate.

The play ends, as the ball is relayed to the infield, and I glance up, and our lead runner is within 5 feet of me, standing nonchalantly on third base. I do a double take looking at him, and the first thing out of my mouth is, "What are you doing here? I waved you in to score about five minutes ago!" Which I had. And he says, "Coach, you said 'Hold up.' I heard you say, 'That's good right there.'"

Well, what happened was that the lead runner saw and heard his verbal and hand signal to keep running. I waved him home, pointed at home plate, and yelled, "Score, Score!" which is our command. But I kept standing in the same place and began yelling immediately to the trail runner to hold up. Well, the lead runner followed my initial direction to keep running and head for home, but when he heard me hollering to the trail runner to hold up, he thought I meant this for him. He was halfway down the line already, could have walked home and scored, but he did just what he thought he was told, and ran back to third base.

Again, communication is the key to success. What I should have done was wave the lead runner in to score, then sprint back toward third base as I began delivering verbal and hand signals to the trail runner. Then, the lead runner would have passed out of earshot and continued his sprint toward home plate. This was the first time this ever happened to me coaching third, and it occurred in the biggest game of the year. Isn't that always the way? Fortunately, our leadoff hitter hit a line drive single up the middle and scored both runners, so my communication problems with our lead runner rounding third didn't cost us a run or the ball game.

But it taught me to incorporate a new drill into our practice baserunning routines. We put runners on first and second and had a coach hit balls into the gaps in the outfield, and practiced communicating with the lead and trail runners receiving different commands. We never had this problem in an actual contest again after we began practicing this part of the game.

Practice Like You Play

This is a classic example of "Practice the things that happen in a game." Everything you do in practice should emanate from and mirror live game situations. If it doesn't occur in a game, forget spending time practicing it. If it does occur in a game, you've got to create a drill or figure out a way to

*Figure 7. **Communicating with multiple runners on the same play.** The third base coach learns early to leave his box and provide a good visual angle for the runner. With multiple runners, get the first one waved, leave him and sprint back to the bag to signal any trail runners. I've miscommunicated and wound up with two runners occupying third base simultaneously, one retreating and one advancing. If that happens and you're the third baseman, tag 'em both, just to be sure. By rule, the lead runner has the right to the bag and the trail runner should be tagged, but who can think that fast?*

communicate successfully with your players in practice, through repetition, what is physically expected of them in actual games.

***

We always spent one entire, early season practice talking only about baserunning. If you cover everything you should, it will take most of your daylight. It is the one time during the spring team practice regimen when you will eschew the practice organization philosophy of "one minute to talk, 10 minutes to drill." It's that important. Baserunning mistakes will kill you, and a smart baserunning ball club has such an advantage over its opponents. Truthfully, it's the one area of the game that is most ignored by high school coaches. Ask a typical head coach, "How much time and how many drills are allotted each day solely to baserunning?" and the answer is likely to be "None."

Yet, how often in high school games does a player fail to make a "heads-up" baserunning play that could have garnered him an extra base and perhaps led to an extra run? Moreover, how often does a player make a baserunning error that kills a rally and keeps a team from maximizing its offensive chances? The answer to both questions is, of course, frequently.

As much as I coveted speed on the base paths, I must say, in all honesty, that speed on defense saved us more runs than speed on offense created for us. Well, you know by now how much I emphasized speed and aggressive baserunning. But defensive speed, especially in the outfield, will win games for you. Say the opposition has the bases loaded and their no. 3 hitter hits a smash deep and long into the right field gap. Now say you're playing a first round tournament game hosted on a college campus, and that the host school has a big ballpark. Lots of space in the alleys and lots of distance to the fence. So if the ball is not caught in the air, it is pretty certain that all three baserunners will score. And they may think about trying to wave the batter-runner as well. You're cringing in the dugout, watching the ball flight and the runners poised to take off, when your centerfielder races over and somehow backhands the ball in the air. He then jumps up and pegs a perfect relay to your second baseman, who races into the infield with the ball before one base in taken by the opposition. Your centerfielder has just saved you three, maybe even four runs, on one play. With excellent baserunning techniques, you can take an extra base, and ignite rallies, and find a way to score when the bats are silent, but it's hard to match that defensive contribution to a game in one fell swoop.

Speaking of great outfield catches and playing in big ballparks reminds me of an incident that occurred when I was coaching in Texas. Our centerfielder that year was about as good as they come and by mid-season already had a highlight reel of amazing catches to his credit. We're playing in a tournament game in a huge college ballpark, with lots of pro scouts in attendance. Joe Pittman, a scout with the Astros, comes down to our dugout before the game and says, "Got anybody I should look at?" And so I say, "I think barring injury our centerfielder has a chance to be an everyday player in the bigs." Joe wrinkles up his face, doesn't even ask the kid's name. I know he doesn't believe me, and that's fine. Coaches oversell players all the time, so he thinks I'm a phonus balonus.

The game starts, and right away, top of the first, their no. 2 hitter pulls a long drive to right center. This ball is really powdered. Everyone looks at the ball and the position of the outfielders and does the angles and the math with their eyes and figures, well, this is at least a triple, and maybe four bases. It's a big, big park. Well, the ball is really carrying, but as it rises through the air in the alley, you can see our centerfielder closing the gap on it. This is the kid that we timed in under three seconds home to first on a batted ball. He was a whirling dervish out there in center: There just wasn't anything hit in the air that he didn't think he could make a play on. He had natural style and panache, too. Often, at the crack of the bat, and on pure instinct, he would grab his cap off the top of his head with his throwing hand, Willie Mays style, and run the ball down carrying his cap in his hand. I tell you, he was fun to watch. What a player he was!

Anyway, he closes the gap on this long smash and at the very last second reaches up and pulls it down. Whirls and throws back to the infield like it was nothing and starts to jog back toward dead center. There's a ripple going through the ballpark, and you can hear people saying, "Did you see that?" and "How did that happen?" About two seconds after the ball is returned to the infield Joe Pittman is pulling on my shoulder and saying intensely, "What did you say this kid's name was?" I laughed and told him and took Joe's card and promised to email him contact information. The Astros ended up drafting him in the second round that spring.

So there's no substitute for speed and quickness on defense, and I'll be the first to admit it. But you've got to score runs on offense to win, and that's what we're here to talk about.

Coaching Your Hitters (and Baserunners)

Your hitters should be coached, prior to the first pitch of every at bat, to remain completely out of the box until they get their sign. On each subsequent pitch, the hitter must check with you again. Coach your right-handed hitters to leave their back foot, or right foot, planted in the box, and to open up with the left foot and step out of the box toward third base with their left foot to see you and get the sign. Then when the sign is received, the hitter steps back in with his left foot, without having to replant his right foot. Your left-handed hitters will have to step out of the box completely between each pitch, get their sign, then step back in and resettle both feet in the box.

Figure 8. Hitters should check the third base coach on every pitch. Right-handed hitters can leave the back foot planted when taking a sign. Lefties should get out of the box quickly with both feet in between each pitch and then resettle into their hitting stance.

If they don't, they could be vulnerable to a quick pitch, so they've got to get out of the box completely to pick up a potential sign.

This sounds time consuming, but if you coach your baserunners and hitters well, everybody can be on the same page in a matter of two or three seconds between each pitch, and boom, your hitter is back in the box ready to hack, and your baserunners are on the sack with sign intact, ready to take their primary lead. It is imperative that your hitters and baserunners perform this small procedure on every pitch. If you have to yell your hitters' and baserunners' names and get their attention, then flash a bunt sign, you might as well take out an ad in the local paper that says, "Hey, we're putting a play on now!"

Your hitters must step out in this fashion on every pitch, in summer ball, fall ball, intrasquad games, every time they play representing your team. It must become second nature to them. Your baserunners must bust it back to the bag after every pitch is successfully received, and immediately pick up the same sign you're delivering to your hitter, at the same time. You always want to deliver your signs to your hitter and your baserunners simultaneously. This is strategic communication, and it must be done this way. You get multiple runners on base and fail to have a coordinated sign delivery system in place, you're going to have some problems putting a play on. Everybody's got to be on the same page, at the same time. It's got to become second nature on every pitch for batters and baserunners alike.

First baserunning session of the year, emphasize to your team that they will sprint to first on a walk or on a hit-by-pitch. This complements your aggressive mindset, and allows the baserunner(s) and batter to communicate quickly before the defense has even begun to attempt to analyze your signals.

Now, walk the team toward first, and halfway down the line you show your team the runner's lane in foul territory, and explain that a runner can be called out if while running to first he is judged to have interfered with a throw from another player to first base. Technically, your runner can be called out if he interferes with the defense's ability to make a play, even if the ball doesn't hit him. This interference is usually caused by the runner veering out of the runner's box and into fair territory.

As the team stands at the home plate end of the runner's lane, have a coach demonstrate visually and verbally two commands: "Beat it out" and "Go for two." If the coach yells "Beat it out," he will be pointing at the first base bag. If he yells "Go for two," he will be windmilling with his left arm and pointing toward second base with his right.

If the coach is pointing at first base and yelling "Beat it out," the player runs through the runner's lane to first base. Walk to first, and explain that the bag is in fair territory, and how to run through it without lunging. Tell your players to always run through the bag with their normal strides, unless a throw has pulled the first baseman off the bag and they can clearly see that he is going to need to tag them to get them out. Then explain to your players that a head first slide is appropriate, and show them how to slide in the runners' lane while reaching for the bag with the left hand.

Now walk back down halfway to home plate. Have your first base coach point to second base and yell "Go for two." Here, you demonstrate how to widen out into the grass and make a semi-circular, rounded turn at first base, pushing off the corner of the bag closest to the pitcher's mound to propel yourself in a direct line toward second base.

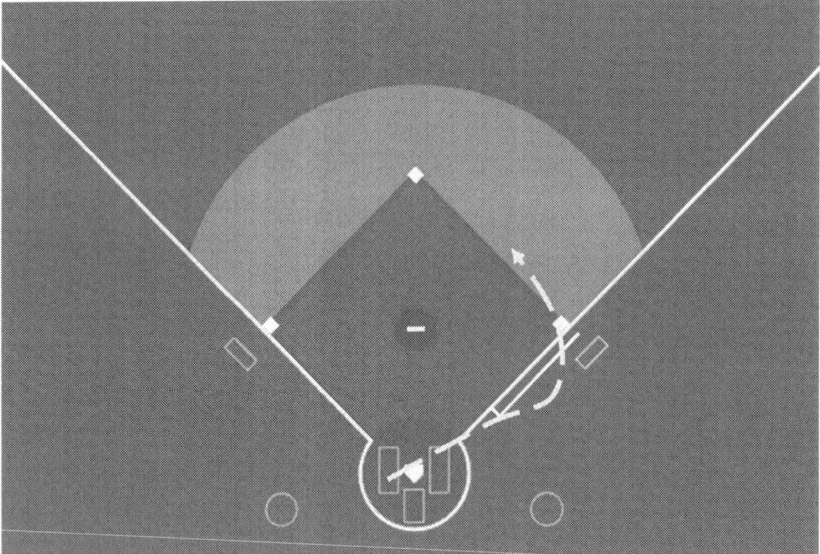

*Figure 9. **Beat it out or go for two.*** *When the batter-runner reaches the runner's lane and sees the first base coach waving him toward second and hollering "Go for two," he should execute a small semi-circle toward the first base dugout and then push off the inside part of the first base bag in a direct line toward second base.*

Now walk your team down the foul line past first base, and explain the rule regarding a player making a movement toward second base once he has passed first base.

Technically, if your runner stops at first base, as on a walk or hit by pitch, for example, he is fair game if he strays from the base at any time after his initial contact with it.

But on a batted ball, the runner is allowed by rule to sprint through and overrun the bag and return safely to the base without being tagged out, if he has not made a discernable movement toward second base. Now, say your runner sprints through the bag on a close play at first. And that the ball trickles away from the first baseman. If upon seeing this, your runner makes one movement, or takes one step toward second, suddenly he becomes "live" and can be tagged out if the defense can put a tag on him before he returns to the bag.

Rules allow your runner to turn toward the infield, rather than toward foul territory, and return safely to the bag, as long as he makes no attempt to advance to second. However, to insure that the umpire makes the

Figure 10. Communication is the key to success. Both fists up means "nobody out." The runner flashes a similar sign back to the third base coach. Baserunning decisions are often determined by how many outs there are. If we're in a 0-0 game in the top of the second inning, and you're on first base with nobody out when the hitter behind you rips one into the gap, you may get held at third. After all, there are three more chances to score you. If there are two out and there's a ball in the gap, you better be moving and not stop until you reach the dugout.

correct call, I advise you to coach your runners to always turn to the right and then return to the bag. Then there can be no doubt in the umpire's mind that your runner made no attempt to advance to second. Yasiel Puig was called out on this same play the other day in a Dodgers' game, without having made a move toward second. He just turned that way and looked in.

Say your guy sprints through the bag on a close play, sees the ball get away from the first baseman, and makes a quick movement toward second base before deciding that he cannot advance. It happens. Now he is fair game to be tagged out. But he has the advantage of running anywhere he wants to in order to get back to first and avoid a tag. Teach your runners that if this happens, they can run into the infield, or move into foul territory, or play "Catch me if you can" in any form or fashion they choose in getting safely back to first base. Teach them to dive headfirst back into first base if they have to; it's an unusual play, somewhat similar to a catcher chasing a runner around home plate after the runner has attempted to score and failed to touch the plate.

One year we had our first baseman assume his "stretch and receive" position at first, had a coach throw the ball past first as if it got away from the first baseman, and then had a "live" baserunner attempt to get back to first after turning the wrong way on the overthrow. The two kids played a game of tag for several seconds, the team hollered and had a little fun, and you can rest assured they never forgot the rule.

Okay. Your runner is safe at first. Now you demonstrate how he must show you (you're standing in the third base coaching box) the number of outs.

Coach your players to run full speed to first (yes, even on a walk) and occupy the bag immediately and turn to the third base coach immediately. Your baserunners should be coached to reach that bag full speed, determine that they can't advance any further (we'll talk about that momentarily), and immediately signal to you the number of outs with their hands. With nobody out, the baserunner holds up two fists; with one out, he holds up one hand with his ring finger pointed skyward; and with two outs, the baserunner shows you the "Hook 'em Horns" sign with both hands.

While your players are participating in the drill, one of your coaches is watching carefully to make sure that all the runners are sprinting in foul territory toward first base. Should a player veer inside the foul line, the coach should stop the drill and instruct the player to return to the batter's box and run again in foul territory.

Now, this chapter is not intended to serve as a rules session, but things get complicated on the bases, as we will discuss momentarily. By teaching your players the rules regarding baserunning early in your pre-season practices, you will avoid confusion and unnecessary outs later in the year.

Knowing the Rules

How important is it for your baserunners to know the rules? True story here. We're playing a huge district game in Georgia against a traditional powerhouse. Both teams are undefeated in district play and the winner will gain an edge in the push for the playoffs.

We're down 2-1 in the fourth inning and our leadoff hitter comes up to start the inning and singles to center. He takes his lead off first, and on the first pitch, our no. 2 hitter, a lefty, slices a long, high fly ball to left. The ball really drifts and carries and the left fielder goes way back, almost to the fence, to await its downward flight. Meanwhile, our leadoff hitter, who can fly, has taken off with the crack of the bat and is having trouble locating the ball. He's so fast that he's on second almost immediately and rounds it and holds up about five or six steps past second.

Our runner either locates the ball, or what's happening dawns on him (he never picked me up visually in the third base coach's box), and as he sees that the ball may be caught, he starts retreating. Now the left fielder is making a play on the ball in the air, and we're all yelling at our baserunner to "Get Back!" So our baserunner finally sees the need to return to first. He turns back as if to head toward second, but then cuts through the dirt on the home plate side of second, making a direct line back to the base path between first and second, and he never retouches second base. Which of course by rule he is required to do.

Now, about this time, the left fielder sees that he may have an opportunity to throw to first and double off our baserunner, because our runner has advanced so far on the fly ball. So he uncorks a huge throw that sails over the cutoff man's head, gets by the first baseman, and skips out of play, rattling around in the first base dugout.

Is the runner out automatically because he didn't retouch second immediately? Did the ball being thrown out of play, which would advance the runner two bases, overrule his baserunning mistake? What the heck is the correct ruling? A 10 minute confab/rhubarb ensued. The opposing coach argued that the runner should have been out immediately upon bypassing second base and not retouching it, regardless of the fact that his team threw the ball out of play. I argued that that there's no way to know that the runner wouldn't have returned to retouch second, and that the ball being thrown out of play should give the runner two bases and that he should occupy third. After all, doesn't the runner retain the right to return and touch second later in the play?

Here's what I mean. Let's say your leadoff guy hits a triple, but misses second base in his haste to get to third. After your runner had rounded second and moved halfway between second and third, you get his attention and wave him back to touch second. That happens, right? So, I argued, what's the difference here? Our runner might have returned and touched second. There's no way for the umpires, or anyone else for that matter, to know that he wouldn't. And the ball was thrown out of play before he had returned all the way to first.

After a wild argument and lengthy deliberation, the home plate ump finally ruled that our runner was out and that the throw was irrelevant. His ruling was that the instant the baserunner failed to retouch second on his way back to first, he must be called out. I didn't get it, and I'm still not sure I do, even though I've revisited the rule numerous times. I think the field ump was with me, too, but the home plate ump made the ruling. And it stood.

Now we've got one out and nobody on, and we end up not scoring in the inning. We lost 4-3 and our opponents went on to capture the district championship. I still believe that if I had taken the time to cover this rule with our players early in the season that this one play may have made the difference in the ball game, and thus the difference in the district race. Who knows? Point is, the better coached team has an advantage.

Primary and Secondary Leads

While you're at first base, demonstrate to your team how to take a primary and secondary lead off first base, how to initiate the straight steal of second, and how to execute the delayed steal of second base.

First, have a player demonstrate the proper technique for assuming a primary lead. The player stands to the infield side of first base, with the side of his left foot touching the bag. He remains there, touching the bag, until the pitcher actually contacts the rubber. Put a pitcher on the mound at this point in practice, and have him throw to a catcher from the stretch, and demonstrate to your players that the pitcher, after receiving the return throw from the catcher, will frequently walk around the mound, check baserunners, go to the resin bag, or communicate with infielders before re-contacting the rubber. While this is occurring, the runner at first should remain in contact with the bag. Emphasize to your players that there is no need to make yourself a target for an out in between pitches by being off the bag.

Once the pitcher re-contacts the rubber and looks in for his sign, the baserunner should take four crablike, sideways steps toward second base, while keeping his eyes focused completely on the pitcher's back. The baserunner steps four times to the right, shuffle style, without ever crossing one foot over another, so that at no time can he be caught in a crossover movement by a quick pickoff throw: feet apart, feet together, feet apart, feet together, four times. His right or lead foot should be about 10-12 feet off first base. After taking four sideways steps, the baserunner remains crouched in an athletic position, with his hands dangling loosely in front of him, just as if he's an infielder prior to a pitch. Many coaches like their baserunners to concentrate on the front or left heel of a right-handed pitcher, because this heel must initiate a turn toward first base if a pickoff throw is coming. I didn't obsess about this point. If the baserunner was comfortable just looking at the pitcher's back, that was fine with us. We will talk baserunning versus a left-hander shortly.

Now, have your pitcher come set in his stretch while your runner has assumed his primary lead. Then have your pitcher go home with the ball. The microsecond that your pitcher shows that he is going home (and not initiating a pickoff move), your baserunner should execute his secondary lead. This involves two long, sideways, shuffle jumps on the balls of the feet and directly in the base path in a straight line toward second base, while the runner maintains his posture, looking in to home plate. The baserunner should be taught to cover as much ground as possible in these two sideways shuffle jumps, while lifting his feet off the ground in a minimal fashion. In other words, he wants to move sideways, not up.

He will land from his second shuffle jump about the time the ball reaches home plate, and he will prepare to crossover with his left foot and punch with his left arm to react to a wild pitch, passed ball, or downward contact ground ball and in so doing will be turned and sprinting toward second. He must also be prepared to use his right foot and leg as a springboard to throw himself back toward first base, if and when the catcher handles the ball cleanly. Here's the rub. He's got to be prepared to move quickly either way.

Most times, the catcher will handle the pitch cleanly, in which case you want your baserunner "to bust it back to the bag." If the catcher throws behind your runner at first, and your runner can return to first standing up, he doesn't have a big enough combination of primary and secondary lead. We also coached the same thing on a pitcher's pickoff throw. If our runner didn't have to dive back on a pitcher's pickoff attempt, he didn't have a large enough primary lead. Let's say there was a pickoff attempt and our runner went back into first base standing up. We would immediately give him the "widen your lead" hand signal, which is two palms together and then move the palms far apart.

Moving aggressively the other way is just as important. To advance to second on a ball that dribbles away from the catcher (and there's a lot of these in high school baseball), you've got to take a healthy secondary lead on every pitch. Baserunners who lean back toward the previously occupied base as the ball reaches the catcher are at a decided disadvantage if they attempt to advance on a ball that gets away from the catcher. They've got to plant, stop, and reverse direction and then regain momentum heading toward second. The player who takes a strong secondary lead can just crossover, punch, and go. It's often the difference between being called out and safe at second base. Many games have turned on less, so I strongly urge you to emphasize the importance of a secondary lead. You see poorly executed secondary leads at every level of baseball. It's more understandable at the professional level, because such a vast majority of pitches are handled cleanly, and the runner is nearly always returning to the previously occupied bag. But in high school, if your baserunners diligently practice and execute strong secondary leads, and moving to the next base on balls that escape the catcher, you'll be amazed at how many extra bases they can take.

Watch a high school game and take special notice of runners taking a walking lead off third base. When the ball actually arrives at the plate, which direction is the runner actually moving? Eight times out of 10, you'll see the runner come down the line toward home during the pitcher's windup, but begin moving back toward third at the exact time the catcher receives the ball. So, if there's a ball that's not handled cleanly by the catcher, and the runner wants to attempt to take home, he's got to replant, reverse his momentum, and throw himself back in the direction of home plate. This is the reason why it's so important for your baserunners to actually be moving toward the next base as the ball is received by the catcher, still committed to their secondary lead. If this takes them too far down the line, instruct them to shorten their primary lead. But the secondary lead gives you momentum and allows you to score, because you're already moving in that direction. Now if your players execute the secondary lead properly and the catcher handles the pitch cleanly, they've really got to reverse hard and bust it back to the bag. Which is course why that part of baserunning must be emphasized as well. You maximize your primary and secondary leads, then if the ball if handled cleanly, you come back hard to the previous bag. Every pitch, every time.

Combination Drill

Alright, here's a combination drill with lots of options. With a pitcher on the mound and a catcher behind home plate and a first baseman holding, have a baserunner prepare to take his primary lead off first. Add two more players in a direct line behind the first baserunner in the outfield side dirt of the infield. Place two "throwdown" rubber bases touching the foul line and directly behind first base, so that the two players behind the "live" runner have a base to lead from and come back to. (Buy some throwdown rubber bases. They are inexpensive and can serve as an excellent logistical aid in extending baserunning drills.)

Figure 11. Practice the art of baserunning and defense simultaneously. Utilize a third runner with a third throwdown base, a catcher and two middle infielders, and work primary leads, secondary leads, busting it back to the bag, straight steal, delayed steal, and ball in the dirt reaction.

Now, have the pitcher contact the rubber and have all three baserunners take their primary lead. The pitcher takes his stretch and will, three times out of four, go home with the ball. When the baserunners determine that the pitcher is indeed going home, they execute their secondary lead. Then, when the ball is handled cleanly by the catcher, they "bust it back to the bag." Once in every few reps, have the pitcher throw over to first, practicing his pickoff move. If any of the baserunners return to the bag standing up, work with them on taking a larger primary lead. Study the players' secondary leads and stop the drill and demonstrate the proper secondary lead action if necessary. Remember, two long sideways, shuffle jumps by the baserunner as soon as the pitcher goes home with the ball. And keep the momentum headed toward second until the runner is absolutely certain that the pitch has been handled cleanly.

Now, give a nod to your catcher, and continue the drill (have the baserunners change lines, so that everyone gets a chance to be "live" one-third of the time) with the catcher practicing throwing behind the runner to first base about every three or four throws. So now you've got the pitcher working his pickoff move, the catcher throwing behind the runner, and the baserunner working on his primary and secondary leads and "busting it back to the bag."

Now add the third element of the drill. Have a coach stand beside the catcher with a handful of baseballs. Every fourth or fifth pitch, as the catcher cleanly handles the pitcher's throw, have your coach roll the ball lightly out behind home plate, as if the catcher has mishandled the ball. The coach can tell the catcher prior to the pitch "Rolling one," and the catcher will know to receive the pitch, but to turn and move as if to chase after a "mishandled ball." The baserunners are coached to react to the "rolled ball" by the coach as if it is a passed ball, and must convert their secondary lead into a sprint for second base. All three baserunners will react by finishing the second hop of their secondary lead and run full speed through the bag or through the space behind the bag (for the two players who are not "live"). I don't recommend having the "live" baserunner slide into second, even during practices prior to opening day. The risk for injury is just too high.

You can also add middle infielders to the drill. And you can have the coach roll the ball a few feet to the left and right of the catcher, in foul and/or fair territory, making it possible for the catcher to have a play on the advancing runner. Prior to the pitch, your middle infielders can practice signaling to one another as to who will cover second should the runner attempt to advance. After the trio of baserunners has sprinted through second base, have them jog around behind shortstop on the short grass in left and continue jogging behind third base and home plate until they return to the baserunners' group at first base.

Walking It Up

This sounds elementary, but one of the first things you should do when teaching baserunning is to coach your players how to "walk it up" on the bag after diving back into the base without getting tagged out. You'd be astounded at how many times I have seen players get tagged out because even though they stole a base or dived back into one successfully, they failed to maintain contact with the bag while moving from a prone position to a standing position.

Here's what you do. Have your players lie face down near first, second, and third base as if they have just rounded the base and dived back into the bag. Have them stretch out and touch the bag with one hand. (You can use throwdown bases behind all three real bases and work nine players simultaneously.) Now, have the player carefully pull himself toward the bag, while maintaining contact with the base with his other hand, and then bend up with one knee and put one foot on the bag, all the while maintaining contact with his hand. Then have the player release contact with his hand and move to a full standing position.

The verbal command should be "Walk it up, walk it up," which means stay in contact with the bag as you reassume a standing position.

To add flavor to the drill, have an infielder with the ball in his glove apply a fake tag to the player while he's prone in the dirt, then have the infielder attempt to tag the runner out as he "walks it up." This will teach the baserunner to remain in contact at all times with the bag.

Utilizing the Stopwatch and Picking Your Spots

I'm not a gizmo guy, but a stopwatch should be standard equipment on your uniform and on the uniform of your other coaches.

A very good time for pitchers, from the moment they break the set position until the ball reaches the catcher's glove, is 1.2 seconds. Usually that's on a fastball.

A really good time for a throw from the catcher to second base, "pop to pop" or glove to glove, is 2.0 seconds. That's under game conditions, with the catcher handling a ball that is not in the dirt and not disrupting his step and throw movement.

So combine these two times, and you've got a total of 3.2 seconds to get your baserunner from the apex of his primary lead at first to making contact with second base on a steal. Now, that's against a fastball, and against a pitcher, catcher, and defense that executes extremely well. Against a pitchout, you may only have 3.0 seconds. Running against a breaking ball, or against a pitcher who is slow to the plate out of the stretch, or against a catcher who doesn't throw well, you will obviously have more time.

If your baserunner, at the apex of his lead off first, is 4 yards or 12 feet off the bag, which he should be, he has to cover 78 feet, or 26 yards, in 3.2 seconds to arrive at second in concert with the baseball. He has to get there in 3.1, we might surmise, to beat a well-coordinated defensive effort.

Thus, it is imperative that you work with your baserunners on taking as large a lead as possible off of first base without getting picked. And it's equally important that you work with them constantly on "punching" toward second with the left fist and pivoting and crossing over with the left leg on that first explosive movement toward second base.

Every practice, work your baserunners three at a time leading off first against "live" pitchers on the mound. Obviously, you can work your defense simultaneously. Stress to your runners that their eyes must remain on the pitcher at all times, and that their foot movements should be automatic, side-to-side shuffle steps, and never crossover steps. Have them work on maximizing their lead, then the punch and crossover and sprint toward second when they recognize that the pitcher is going home with the baseball. More on the execution of the straight steal in the next chapter.

Time them in their sprint to second. If they are much over 3.3 seconds through the bag at second, you've got to get them to be quicker. If, however, they can get through the bag in 3.3 or less most of the time, the defense is going to have to be awfully good to stop your steal of second.

During the off-season, work plyometrics and other jumping exercises that develop the explosive muscle movements. Your guys don't have to run a long way, they just have to run relatively short distances in a short burst.

When you have tryouts, time your guys in the 30-yard dash and the 25-yard dash. This is bag to bag with no lead, and extended lead to the next bag. The guys who cover this distance may not be your best at 100-yard sprints or even at 60-yard sprints, but they will steal you some bags. And if coached properly to executive secondary leads when they're not taking off on a straight steal, they will have a good chance of taking the next base on a ball that bounces away from the catcher or a ball in the dirt of any kind.

In high school, not many opposing pitchers will work from their stretch in any of their eight warm-up tosses on the mound prior to the first inning, so normally you can't time them before the game from breaking the stretch to fastball reaching the catcher's mitt. However, most high school pitchers will work from the stretch a few times in the bullpen while they're warming up. Nothing wrong with getting your break to glove time there.

Most catchers will throw to second at the end of their pitcher's pre-game warm-ups on the mound. Time that throw from catcher's glove to middle infielder's glove, or "pop to pop."

Then, of course, you want to time the pitcher's movement to home plate the first time there's a baserunner and he works from the stretch. And of course time the catcher on his first "live" throw to second on an attempted steal. Have three stopwatches operable at all times: one on the pitcher, one on the catcher, and one to record home to first times on batted balls for your players when you are at bat. Hopefully, by the second inning or so, you'll have a pretty good idea of what you're up against, in addition of course to what your eyes tell you.

Now, if a kid has an excellent fastball, and throws it a lot, it's going to be harder to run on him than it is on a pitcher who uses more off-speed stuff. Sometimes a kid is slow to the plate, but runs it up there in a hurry, and offsets his slow movement with a 90 mph heater. The Orioles, who have had a world of 20-game winners, did a fascinating study and came up with the statistic that they had never had a 20-game winner who didn't throw at least 60% fastballs. It's still the best pitch in the game and sets up all other pitches. Harder to run against, too.

As we mentioned, sometimes teams will pitch out on you, especially early in the game, if just to show you that they will and plant that seed of caution in your mind. We always liked to run on the next pitch after a pitchout. Rarely will a high school coach call two pitchouts in a row. And it's an aggressive, "you can't stop us by pitching out" mentality.

Truly, though, the best time to run is on an off-speed pitch, especially a slow-breaking curve. They take a while to reach home plate, they are handled cleanly by the catcher less frequently, and they often wind up in the dirt. You and your baserunners and your entire ball club must study each pitcher you face and decipher his pitching pattern. When does he throw his breaking ball?

Many high school pitchers only throw their curve ball when they're ahead or even in the count. So if your hitter is down 0-1 in the count after a first pitch fastball, and you're pretty sure this guy's pattern is to throw the deuce now that he's ahead, that's the time to run. Study the guy. What does he throw 3-2? Will he ever use his curveball then? What does he throw first pitch? Will he vary his pitch selection according to the lineup? Throw a first pitch change up to your no. 3 hitter? Throw a 3-2 curveball to your no. 4 hitter? Or will he rare back and challenge you with heat when he gets behind.

The toughest pitchers to read and thus to run on are those more sophisticated pitchers who "pitch backwards," guys who throw their breaking stuff when they're behind and who throw and/or spot the fastball when they're ahead. It takes confidence for a young pitcher to throw his deuce on a 3-1 count, or even a 2-1 count, because theoretically the fastball is easier to control. Hitters are trained to look "fastball" when the pitcher is behind in the count 2-0 and 3-1, and there's a reason for that.

For those baserunners and rabbits who are "green-lighted," make sure they understand the advantage of running on off-speed pitches and how to look for them. And make sure that you and your coaches are using those stopwatches.

The Ultimate Combo Baserunning-Team Defense Drill

If forced to name one drill that I found most beneficial for our entire team over the course of my coaching career, I would pick the following combination baserunning-team defense drill. It involves placing baserunners at second and third, a batter-runner at home plate, and a coach hitting fungoes to a full defensive squad. Here's how it works. Both the baserunners and the batter runner and the defense play each fly ball off the coach's bat as if there's nobody out, and they play each base hit ground ball base hit as if there's two outs.

You start with a pitcher on the hill. He can work from the windup or the stretch, but either way, the runners on second and third take primary leads.

The ball is received by a catcher in full gear, who tosses it behind him to a shagger. As the catcher receives the pitch, you hit a fungo to the outfield. As the ball is released by the pitcher, the baserunners take their secondary leads and then react to the ball being hit by the coach. The batter-runner at home plate reacts as if he has hit the ball himself to the outfield and makes his sprint toward first base.

First, let's assume the coach hits a fly ball to the outfield. Okay, that means there's nobody out and the defense must figure this on their own. After a day or two of practicing this drill, they'll get the hang of it. The runner on third practices busting it back to the bag and preparing to tag up and race for home. If it's deep enough, he tries to score. If it's not, after the catch in the outfield he runs far enough down the line to draw a throw and hopefully entice the defense into making a throwing mistake, then returns to the bag.

The defense plays it "live." If the ball is caught shallow enough so that the defense has a legitimate play at home on the runner tagging up at third, the outfielder practices "running through the catch" and throwing "through the cutoff man" toward home plate. Your cutoff man makes the decision, while listening to the catcher, to cut the throw or let it fly. Your trail runner at second base tags up and either attempts to advance or makes the decision not to, depending on where and when the throw arrives in the infield. If the defense can't get the lead runner, they may make a play on the trail runner.

Say the ball was hit to the left fielder. In that scenario, with a play at the plate, the third baseman is the cutoff man, so the shortstop covers third, right? So if the catcher hollers "Cut 3" rather than "Leave it fly," the third baseman cuts the ball and throws to the shortstop covering third to nab the trail runner there. Same scenario if the ball is fielded by the centerfielder or rightfielder; only then the first baseman becomes the cutoff man, right? Meanwhile, the batter runner sprints toward first and reacts to the play.

If the ball is caught in the air, he is out and returns to the runners' line near home plate. If the outfield bungles the play, he attempts to advance as far as he can.

Now, if the ball is hit deeper, but is still catchable by the outfield, the defense adjusts during the ball flight. Knowing that they can't make a play on the lead runner tagging up at third and coming home, they reconfigure for a play at third base. Say the ball is hit deeper and to center field. The shortstop moves out onto the grass, in a direct line between the centerfielder and third base, to set up as a relay man for the throw to third. Now the defense's focus becomes preventing the trail runner from advancing to third, and of course, the intent of the trail runner is to tag up and take third successfully. Normally we don't have our baserunners slide, we just have them run through the bag at third and through the plate at home to avoid collisions and injuries.

Okay. Now say your coach slaps a ground ball base hit into the outfield or a line drive base hit into the outfield. Everyone automatically assumes now that there are two outs. You don't tell the defense, they just "learn" from repeating this drill that a ground ball base hit means there's two outs. The lead runner on third sets off for home as soon as he reads "downward contact" or base hit, knowing that there are two outs and that he should try to score on virtually anything. And of course he scores and then gets back in line with the other baserunners near home plate. With two outs, you want your trail runner at second trying to score on just about anything in a game, right? So he's got to try to score in this drill.

Another good combo aspect of this drill is that the defense and the batter-runner are a secondary but vital part of this play. The defense must make the decision as to whether to set up for a play at the plate to try to get the trail runner trying to score from second, or to set up for a play at second base, in order to keep the batter-runner from advancing to second base. Normally the defense will set up for a play at the plate, then the catcher will yell "Cut 2" to the infield cutoff man, either the third baseman or the first baseman, once it's determined that there is no play on the lead runner at home. And the infield cutoff man will cut the throw and then throw to second base instead of home. That said, sometimes the ball is hit deep enough in the alley so that the defense can determine on its own that there will be no play at the plate, and the team defense forgets the trail runner from second base heading home, instinctively foregoing that run based on how long it's taking them to make a play on the ball. In that case, one of your middle infielders will need to set up a relay throw to second base, with the goal being to keep the batter-runner at first. Once in a great while, the defense will need to set up a relay throw to third, if you hit one deep enough in the alley and the batter-runner can fly.

Obviously, the batter-runner has to make some decisions as well, which is one of the reasons that this is such a good baserunning drill. Knowing that there are two out, he definitely wants to get into scoring position at second base, so that he can theoretically score on a base hit in a ball game. But in high school baseball, he's more valuable at third base, even with two outs, as we have discussed in earlier chapters. He can score on a passed ball, wild pitch, base hit, fielding error, or on a bunt base hit. So should be attempt to take third in this drill on what will probably be a close play, and risk making the last out of the inning at third base? Well, let's continue talking.

Adding Flavor to an Already Excellent Drill

You can add flavor to this drill in several ways. One way is to have the coach hitting the fungoes to call out the number of the hitter in the lineup as he hits the ball. Let's say you are hitting the fungoes yourself. You can yell, "Number 2 hitter," and stroke a ball into the outfield. Now the baserunners know that they are running with the knowledge that the next man up to bat is their no. 3 hitter, probably their best hitter. Your more sophisticated baserunners will take less chances trying to stretch the double into a triple, knowing that their team's best hitter is due up next. If you yell, "Number 6 hitter" as you stroke the fungo, the baserunners know that the next hitter up is their no. 7 hitter, and they may want to be more aggressive in considering stretching the double into a triple.

Then again, you may want to tell your rabbits, take all you can get, in any situation, including this one. And damn the torpedoes. If your kids can run, why handicap them? Here's what I mean. Let's say your kid knows there's two outs, and he knows the no. 3 hitter is up next, so he knows trying to take third on this play is not a great percentage play. But let's say you've given him the green light to run on his own earlier in the year, and he can really motor. If he doesn't hesitate, and attempts to take third here with two outs, he may get thrown out. And he will have cost you a chance to have your no. 3 hitter swing the stick with a runner in scoring position (at second base). Of course, there's no guarantee your no. 3 hitter is going to garner a base hit and drive the runner in. If your no. 3 guy is really hot, and the opposition knows it, and your no. 4 guy is not a great hitter, they may pitch around him and park him at the open base at first. Most high school teams will not think this way; this is more for higher levels of baseball, but occasionally, and especially when a team knows your personnel very well, it can happen.

Additionally, and most importantly, your batter-runner attempting to take third base may cause a rushed and poor throw by the outfielder, a dropped ball or poor throw by the relay man, or a botched catch and tag by the third baseman. In other words, you are keeping up that scare, and pressuring the defense. This is the heart of the difference between high school baseball and higher levels. Trying to take third on this play is probably a bad play in college and pro ball. In high school, not so much.

The decision whether or not the batter-runner should attempt to take third has a lot to do with how good the opposing pitcher is. If he's super tough, say he's a dominating, nasty lefty and your no. 3 hitter on deck is a left-handed hitter, the batter-runner is making a good percentage play by trying to take third base on the play. If the guy on the hill is a mediocre righty and your no. 3 hitter, hitting from the left side, is likely to smash anything the pitcher throws up there, it's probably not the best idea to attempt to take third on the play. Isn't baseball wonderful? And high school baseball? There's no game like it, exactly because of situations like these.

Let me just say this, and I'll leave this point alone and move on. Getting your players to think about the risks and rewards of going for third on this play is a gateway to better baserunning and more wins. Talk to your players about why they should consider staying at second and why they must consider going for third base on this play. Stop the drill, have all team members sprint to the infield, and talk about what just occurred. Ask a player who has just attempted to take third base on this play, "What was your thinking there, Scott?" Get a baserunner's dialogue going with your team. Getting them to think about baserunning, and when it's a good percentage play to take a chance and when it's not, is so important. Because it's not what you know, it's what your players know and can apply during games that counts. I've coached against plenty of guys who knew more baseball than me. And a few who knew less. But the goal for you as a coach is not to know more than the next coach, although that helps, certainly. The goal is to communicate more to your players, because they're the ones that must execute on the field. When you reach the point that your players are coaching themselves on the field, and by this, I mean they are making informed, intelligent decisions while racing around the bases, you'll have a dynamite baserunning ball club.

Early in the season, when injuries are not yet such a factor, you can have your pitchers work from the stretch and practice their timing on pickoff plays as part of this same drill. Have the pitcher go home with the ball four or five times in a row, and you fungo to the outfield and put the drill in motion. Then, instead of the pitcher delivering the ball home and you hitting the fungo, have your pitcher throw to second or third with your infielders covering to practice your pre-arranged pickoff plays. Your baserunners at second and third have to dive back, of course, and it keeps them honest.

You can also work in the occasional "throw behind the runner" by the catcher to both bases. This is also "live" teaching, as it forces your baserunners to "bust it back to the bag" after each pitch is successfully received. It keeps your baserunners from "cheating" into bigger primary and secondary leads, and teaches them to sprint back to the bag, or "bust it back to the bag," after every pitch is successfully received. This is how baserunners learn to cover the maximum ground for their primary and secondary leads without getting picked off prior to the pitch or thrown out by the catcher after the pitch is received at home plate.

Figure 12. Make a line drive go through. "Palms flattened" means "freeze on a line drive." The baserunner must be prepared to advance, freeze, or retreat at all times.

One final variation you can add that teaches an excellent baserunning lesson, is to hit the occasional line drive right at one of your infielders, instead of hitting the ball to the outfield. The infielders must react and attempt to make the play on the ball for the out, then attempt to double off the nearest baserunner. Obviously, your baserunners have got to sprint back to the bag to avoid being doubled off. Using this "add on" segment of the drill will teach your baserunners the meaning of "make a line drive go through" better than anything you can verbally tell them. If they get doubled off in this drill because they fell asleep, or were taking too much primary or secondary lead while anticipating the base hit or fly ball to the outfield, you've got a great opportunity for an excellent teaching moment.

The first time one of your baserunners is doubled off second or third when you hit a line drive to the infield instead of hitting a ball to the outfield, suspend the drill temporarily and have all players on offense and defense sprint to the pitcher's mound and take a knee. And say, "Now fellows, watch me and hear me." Then walk over to the third base coaching box and give the "palms down" signal for "watch for the line drive" and simultaneously yell at the team, "Make a line drive go through."

And then return to the pitcher's mound where the team is gathered and say, "Guys, you're gonna' see me make that palms down motion and hear me yell "Make a line drive go through" 3,000 times this year during games. What just happened here in this drill is why you'll get this palms down non-verbal signal and why you'll hear me yell to make the line drive go through. Getting doubled off like we just did will absolutely kill our rally, and it can be avoided by steady and smart baserunning habits. So when we're running this drill here, be alive for the occasional line drive that could double you off, and take your primary and secondary leads without cheating too far. This is why I constantly remind to make the line drive go through."

First time one of your players is picked off, or is thrown out by the catcher throwing behind him after the pitch is received, you may want to consider a similar "quick team instructional meeting" at the mound. And take that opportunity to impart to your baserunners the importance of being aggressive, but being simultaneously studious at avoiding outs. This is the heart of offensive baserunning coaching, and if the message is well received by your players, it can help turn your ball club into a very smart baserunning team.

CHAPTER ELEVEN
STEALING AND
OTHER BASERUNNING PLAYS

"The road has got me hypnotized . . .
and I'm speedin' into a new sunrise."

Radar Love as performed by Golden Earring

Stealing second does many things for your ball club. Most obviously, it puts a guy in scoring position. I'm watching a station-to-station team in the bigs on television recently, and they're struggling at the plate. Guy comes up with two outs and gets a single. Well, the crowd is not unappreciative, but they're not really stirring, because they know the baserunner isn't going anywhere and that it's probably going to take two more hits to score him. Let me ask you. How many times have you seen three consecutive base hits in a ball game, especially with two outs? It just doesn't happen that often. So getting a guy in scoring position is huge.

In high school, you're not only doing that, you're pressuring the defense to make a play that may go awry. The catcher's throw may hit the baserunner in his slide at second and carom off into left center, and the baserunner may jump up and light for third and make it safely. I saw that happen with two outs in a 2-2 SEC game in the eighth inning last weekend. Catcher's throw hit the sliding runner, who hopped up and took third base. Then the next hitter slams one straight down into the turf in front of home plate, and the pitcher has to stand there and wait for the thing to come down.

Meanwhile, the baserunner is off on downward contact, and just beats the pitcher's throw home. They win 3-2.

Your rabbits, your no. 1, 2, 6, 8, and 9 hitters, should practice the straight steal of second every day. All players should practice the "straight steal" mechanics at least twice a week. Players who utilize the delayed steal of second should practice it at least twice a week.

Executing the Delayed Steal of Second

Let's talk about the delayed steal of second, then the straight steal. Essentially, the delayed steal of second is attempted when the runner takes one extra sideways shuffle jump in addition to the two regular shuffle jumps of the normal secondary lead, then takes off for second.

Let's say you've got a righty on the hill contacting the rubber. Your runner takes his crab-like primary lead off first, studying the pitcher as he comes set in his stretch. The pitcher's left heel moves toward third base and home plate, rather than toward first, which means he's going home with the ball. So the runner sees the pitcher going home and takes three sideways hops instead of two, staying low to the ground and hopping more horizontally than vertically, but covering as much ground as possible. Since your runners take two hops with their secondary lead off first on every pitch, the runner taking an extra hop will not sound an alarm bell with the defense.

As you know, middle infielders are trained to glance at the runner at first just as the pitcher is releasing the ball homeward, to see if the runner is stealing. Then they've got to return their attention to the pitch and a possible batted ball. On the straight steal, as the pitcher delivers the ball, the second baseman and shortstop will see the runner turn, pivot, and begin his sprint toward second immediately, eschewing the two hops of the secondary lead. So the coverman will begin his sprint toward second at that exact instant. But here, all the middle infielders see when they glance over to first is the baserunner taking his normal secondary lead.

The catcher also frequently steals a glimpse at the runner just as the pitch is released. He can't focus on the runner, because he's got to play baseball as the pitcher's throw is coming in, but he "senses" the movement of a straight steal. Here, with the delayed steal, the catcher is not alerted as the ball is coming home because oftentimes the baserunner will not complete his third sideways shuffle hop and turn to sprint toward second until the ball is just about at home plate.

So the runner doesn't actually turn, pivot, and sprint toward second base until the baseball reaches the area of the batter's box. Then, he executes the steal as if it is a straight steal play (with the exception of a first and third situation, described below). It's an odd offensive maneuver, because of its timing, and one of the most unique plays in baseball. We stole second so successfully with the straight steal over the years that I did not use the delayed steal very often in my career.

That said, every once in a while you may have a player who embraces the delayed steal and likes to employ it. He may not be one of your fastest players, and may feel like this is his best method of stealing second. One year our catcher, who did not run particularly well, practiced the delayed steal in summer and fall ball and fell in love with it. During our spring high school season he was 7 for 7 taking second on the delayed steal. It's a good weapon to have in your arsenal.

It's got to be practiced, though, if you plan to use it at all, and all your big dogs should drill on the delayed steal twice a week. You normally want your rabbits, or speed guys, to execute the straight steal. Work in groups of three with two throwdown bases against a pitcher, catcher, and first baseman holding, and emphasize covering lots of ground in the three secondary lead hops with long, low jumps.

I like to use the delayed steal with a first and third situation versus a right-hander, and usually with two outs and good speed at third. And a struggling hitter at the plate. This was our version of the old first and third play, where the offense sends the trail runner, and the defense must try to throw him out or execute a play aimed at holding or trapping the lead runner at third, who may try to advance on the throw. With the straight steal, the defense has no choice but to throw through or put a play on, and many times they'll give up the base and just hold the ball to prevent the lead runner at third from breaking for home.

But with the delayed steal, and the runner breaking late, you are more likely to draw a throw. It's more of a challenge to the defense, because you're presenting the possible third out to them and the trail runner looks like easy prey. After all, he's only about halfway to second when the ball gets to home plate. But here's the rub. The catcher may have to throw to a moving target at second. Or sometimes the catcher may throw to second and the coverman isn't there yet at all, because when he peeked over on the pitcher's release the runner on first wasn't moving. The catcher will have the added pressure of knowing that the lead runner at third could possibly score if he throws to second inaccurately, or if he throws through at all.

So many times you get a "held ball' by the catcher on the delayed steal in this situation. And of course, that's not all bad. You haven't scored, but the trail runner takes second standing up, so now you have two guys in scoring position instead of one, and you removed the force play at second.

If the catcher throws to second, and a coverman handles the throw and is there well ahead of the trail runner, you want your trail runner to stop and stay in a rundown as long as possible. The runner on third should break for home the microsecond that the catcher's throw passes the pitcher's mound. If the trail runner sees that he's got a shot at taking second successfully, depending on the reaction of the defense, he should go ahead and sprint full speed and slide, just as he would on a straight steal.

Figure 13. Executing the straight steal. Punch with the left fist to initiate the crossover move that throws your body toward second base. Here, our baserunner employs a low center of gravity and throws the fist to start his acceleration. I think we've got this bag stolen.

THE STRAIGHT STEAL OF SECOND

As we have previously mentioned, on the straight steal of second runners should maximize the primary lead, then punch, crossover, and sprint toward second when they see that the pitcher is going home with the baseball. As the pitch is about to be delivered, the baserunner is at the apex of his primary lead, standing in an athletic position with hands dangling loosely in front of him. The first segment of movement is up top: The baserunner punches the air in a direct line toward second with his left fist. This has the effect of throwing the upper body toward second base and turning the top half of the body in that direction. Simultaneously, the player should also turn on the ball of the left foot and push off toward second, while remaining in a relatively low sprinter's crouch. The player should sprint toward second base, staying in a low, athletic position to maximize speed.

We practice stealing using drills similar to those used in practicing baserunning. Versus a righty, the players should take their normal primary lead with a pitcher on the mound, a catcher behind the plate, and a first baseman holding. Use the triple rotation of baserunners with two throwdown bases behind the real second base bag. After the pitcher contacts the rubber, players should practice their sideways, crab-like, foot-to-foot, shuffle action in taking their primary lead. As soon as the baserunners have recognition (see that the pitcher is going home), they execute a two-part movement in synchronization, performing the straight steal of second and (in practice) running through the bag.

Sliding

When I was a kid I watched an old film clip of the St. Louis Cardinals practicing sliding in a sawdust pit during spring training. So in my first season as a head coach, I organized a "live" sliding drill in the dirt around second base. My starting shortstop injured his ankle and was out for three weeks. Another player bent his ankle backward in an awkward position while sliding in the drill, and he could have been badly hurt. I never practiced "live" sliding again during my career. You can see I'm a quick learner, huh?

Every year, though, I would find a player who either owned or had a younger brother who owned a "slip and slide" plastic mat and I would borrow it early in the season for sliding drills. We'd set it down in the outfield grass between first and second. Players would take their shoes off (no cleats catching in the mat or the ground) and players would stuff their baseball practice pants and even their jerseys with pillowcases and towels and old sweatshirts brought from home. Over the years the players left so many of these articles in our "clothing" bin at the locker room that we eventually developed our own supply of "sliding clothes" and a donated slip and slide mat as well.

A word of caution. If they have to think about it beforehand, some players simply cannot execute a decent practice slide. Avoid worrying about it. We would always have a couple of players who simply could not practice sliding. And we would laugh about it and have them move on to another drill. Now these same players could execute a beautiful hook slide in a game and avoid a tag at a crucial moment. But they did that naturally, without thinking about it, through the application of motor skills and the accumulation of experience over the years. But break it down and ask them to do it in practice, and even in socks and padded soft clothing on a plastic mat, they couldn't do it. Usually it's your more instinctive, natural athletes who have trouble with practicing sliding. It's like hitting. They know how to do it, but they are logjammed if they have to think about what they're doing.

Some players use the hook slide primarily. The hook slide is executed by throwing the feet at the corner of the bag farthest away from "the play," or from the area of the tag. A player stealing second should watch the middle infielder who is covering the bag and slide away from his set-up position. If the middle infielder is reaching toward third base for the ball, the runner should slide toward the right-centerfield corner of the bag. If the infielder was moving to the first base side of the bag to intersect the throw, the runner should "hook" into the pitcher's mound corner of the bag. As the runner's feet slide into the base, normally his legs will continue their momentum slightly and then curl in recoil, so that the player's body ends up looking like a semi-circle. One foot will usually contact the bag, while the other will not be in contact with it. The goal of the hook slide is to avoid a tag. However a player was comfortable doing that was fine with us.

When practicing the hook slide, have a middle infielder mime setting up to take a throw from the catcher, and then have him move to one side of the bag or the other well before the approaching runner arrives. Then the runner's goal, obviously, is to slide to the part of the bag furthest away from the infielder. I preferred not to practice the head-first slide because of potential injuries like jammed wrists and twisted fingers, but oftentimes the players would enjoy the drill so much that they would insist. And many players prefer the head-first slide during games as well.

Again, either was fine with us. We did ask our players to hold a handful of clay in each hand or grasp a batting glove in each hand while on the bases, so that each hand was loosely fisted and not susceptible to finger jams and wrist injuries. It's harder to decelerate on the head-slide, and you can slide by the bag sometimes and offer an easy out to an infielder. But your better players who use the head-first slide will develop a feel for when to start their slide and they'll rarely slide too far. Our best player one year always slid head-first on plays at the plate, and I worried about the catcher coming down on his head or shoulder or arm with heavy, plastic gear. Having a catcher in full regalia plant his shin guard on your head or neck is probably not the best way to stay healthy. But he was good at it, he was comfortable with it, so I never asked him to slide into home feet first.

We taught three slides: the hook slide, the pop-up, and the head-first slide. But I must be honest. We didn't do much instruction with any of these three, other than to demonstrate the classic or proper technique at the onset of the drill. That's because, like batting, sliding is such a unique and individually-styled action. Almost every player has his own sliding style. This is true even in college and the bigs. Very few players slide exactly alike.

And it makes sense that there's a wide variety of styles. Sliding is an unnatural motion for a runner. Try running full speed sometime and then throwing your lower half ahead of your upper body and allowing your feet to drag the ground to slow your momentum. Truthfully, the head-first slide is more comfortable for a lot of players. But we didn't quibble. The players could choose the hook slide or the head-first slide. The only thing we insisted on was using the pop-up slide when appropriate. The pop-up slide is used when a player goes into a slide, sees there will not be a close play, and wants to throw himself back up onto his feet as quickly as possible. In executing the pop-up slide, the player tucks one leg at a 90 degree angle under his top leg, which contacts the bag, and uses the "tucked" underneath leg to propel himself back to his feet after his front leg contacts the bag. You can practice the pop-up slide on the slip and slide matt just like you can the hook and the head-first slide.

STEALING SECOND AGAINST A LEFTY

Players take their primary lead against a left-hander in the same exact way that they do versus a righty. But unless they are stealing on first movement, they may delay their secondary lead until they are sure that the pitcher is going home with the ball.

Running versus a left-hander is not impossible. For as long as high school baseball has been played, 75-85% of lefties on the hill utilize a "typical look": when they are looking directly at the runner at first, they are going home with the ball a vast majority of the time. When they are looking at home plate, they are going to come over to first with a pickoff move a vast majority of the time.

Problems for baserunners emanate from "atypical lefties," or those who utilize a different look or who vary their looks. We loved left-handed pitching, and spent hours and hours working with our lefties on their moves to first. We coached our lefties to look at a spot halfway between first and home on every pitch from the stretch when first base was occupied. And we coached them to roll the stride knee back toward second on their pickoff move, while stepping halfway between home and first after throwing to first.

The rule states that if a left-hander working from the stretch brings his stride foot back past the rubber, he must go home with the ball. But the rulebook doesn't prevent your lefty from rolling his knee. A good move to first by a left-hander is part art and part science. A really, really good move by a lefty can be as valuable as a third or fourth pitch.

Interestingly, most left-handers' moves to first are weaker than right-handers. Why this is I'm not sure. When a lefty has a good move, coach your baserunners to forego taking their secondary lead until they are sure that the pitcher is going home with the ball. This will go a long way toward preventing your runners from getting picked off. If they're stealing, just have them take off on first movement, as we have discussed earlier in the book, and hope to beat the relay throw from first down at second base.

If a lefty has only an average or mediocre move to first, your better baserunners will often be able to "read" him as the game progresses. If they determine that he's "typical," they may be able to run on first movement. And really, in high school baseball, this is not as risky as it sounds. If a lefty is "typical," and he's looking at the runner but planning to go home with the ball, if the runner lights out on first movement oftentimes the pitcher will still not be able to change his motion in mid-stream. In other words, he may actually see the runner breaking for second as he lifts his stride foot, but be incapable of breaking off his motion for home and throwing to first.

Some of your baserunners will be better than others about "reading" a lefty and running on him after he lifts his stride foot. Sometimes they'll be able to communicate a "tell" to the rest of the team. A runner may come to the dugout and say, "If he holds his hands here [he shows an imaginary pitcher holding his hands at his waist in a 'set' motion], he's coming over. If he holds his hands at the letters, he's going home." Sometimes your runners will figure the lefty instinctively and not be able to communicate a "tell" to the rest of the team.

The more lefties your baserunner see, the better they'll be at pressuring them on the bases. Some runners even like working against lefties more, because they're able to look right at them.

LEADING OFF SECOND

Okay, back to our drill. Now after everybody has run through the bag on "Beat it out" or "Go for two" a couple of times, you tell your players to swing the bat in the box, and that everyone will widen out into the grass where the runner's lane starts, and all players will "Go for two." After rounding first base, players are instructed to make visual contact with the third base coach about 15-20 feet on the first base side of second (a coach is standing in the third base coaching box), where the players will either see the "Hold up at second" sign or the "Come on to third" wave.

If they are told to hold up, they round the bag slightly (don't want any players pulling up too sharply and pulling a hamstring), then return to the bag. Then they jog to the outfield grass behind the shortstop's position, round third in foul territory, and come back to home plate, where they take their place in the line again. If they are told to "Come on to third," they continue full speed, round the bag at second while attempting to hit the inside corner of the bag and push off directly toward third base, and sprint to the bag at third. They round the bag slightly at third, return to it, then jog in foul territory to home plate to take their place in the line.

Now have your players practice the two types of leads they will take at second base: a lead with none or one out and the two-out lead.

STRAIGHT LINE AND 2-OUT LEADS OFF SECOND

With nobody out or one out, players should lead off second in a direct line toward third base. With two outs, players should take a "rounded" lead that puts them three or four steps on the outfield grass side of the baseline. This gives them a better angle to "round" third and push off the inside part of third base, propelling them in a direct line toward home plate. The thinking here, of course, is that with two outs, your runner at second base will probably be attempting to score on just about any kind of base hit, whereas with less than two outs, that is not necessarily the case.

You can work your middle infielders and pitchers and practice holding the runner at second and work on pickoffs while your runners are working on proper leads. If you can do this simultaneously without getting anybody hurt, that's good. Early in the year, it's probably more appropriate. Later in the season, when player health becomes even more vital, you may want to work offense and defense separately.

If you are indeed working offense and second base pickoffs simultaneously, include three baserunners in the same drill, just as we did in the "three at once" drill practicing leadoffs and pickoffs at first base. Your "live" runner should take a nobody out or one out lead in a direct line toward third base.

I liked our players to execute a "side straddle" lead at second base, rather than a "walking lead." But both can be effective. We'll talk about both types of leads in a moment.

Stealing Third Base

You occasionally hear baseball people say that it's easier to steal third than second. Perhaps that is because the runner can get a larger or even a walking lead sometimes. Or because the catcher's throw is obstructed with a right-handed batter. However, I never understood that thinking. For one thing, the catcher has a shorter throw to third than he does to second. And his target, the third baseman, is usually closer to the bag than the target he is throwing to at second base. So the catcher is usually throwing a shorter distance to less of a moving target. So all things being equal, I think it's easier to steal second.

STEALING AND OTHER BASERUNNING PLAYS 197

*Figure 14. **Straight line (0 out and 1 out) and 2-out leads from second base.** Practice scoring from second base with a 2-out lead and advancing to third on a ball in the dirt every day. Games are won and lost daily on your ability to do so. When attempting to score from a 2-out lead off second, push off the inside part of the bag and sprint in as direct a line as possible from third base to home plate.*

But pitchers are human. They see baserunners at first much more often than they see runners at second. Thus, they practice holding those runners at second less frequently. So often the baserunner at second can figure the "look" that the pitcher uses on a runner at second, and take off for third after the pitcher has executed the "look" back to second. College programs will work with their pitchers on varying their looks to second when the base is occupied, but high school coaches rarely do. They don't have time and they're overwhelmed as it is. In college ball you've got a pitching coach devoted to helping a pitching staff limit run production. And they take the time to work with their pitchers on holding runners at second.

The two most commonly used "looks," both by righties and lefties, are the "long, slow look," and the "double look." In the first instance, the pitcher will come set, peer in at the catcher, then turn his head and look directly at the runner and "freeze" him until he is ready to turn back toward home and deliver the ball. An astute runner, knowing that the pitcher has only that one move, can accelerate out of his primary lead as soon as the pitcher returns his attention to home plate. Thus, the pitcher becomes known in the dugout as a "one looker." Once runners know this, stealing third is a lot easier. They can take off for third without too much worry as soon as the pitcher ends his long, slow look at second. Many times this is enough jump to steal third.

The problem with using a walking lead from second is that this often tips the pitcher that the runner is on the move. If the pitcher is executing his look to second and sees the runner walking, he may initiate a pickoff play or simply step off the rubber. A walking lead from second is good, in my opinion, only when the pitcher is not executing any look at all, which is very rare. So we liked our runners to lead shuffle-style off of second. Working against a "one looker," a baserunner who executes a shuffle-style lead at second can easily be at full speed with the same kind of punch and crossover step that is taught with the lead off first base.

Stealing third against a "double looker" or "two looker" is a little more problematic, though it can sometimes be easier because the runner can garner a larger lead. Here's what happens. The runner takes his primary lead. The pitcher comes set and looks home, then he glances at second. Then he turns his head back toward home, then back toward the runner a second and final time. Then he'll turn his attention to the plate for good.

For most pitchers, there is a slight delay before they throw home after completing the "second look." If a baserunner takes off for third after the second look, oftentimes he is halfway to third as the pitcher completes his delivery. And he can sometimes steal the bag standing up.

What makes it a little more dicey is that because the pitcher often delays slightly after the second look before he goes home, it gives the catcher and the infielders time to warn the pitcher that the runner is on the move. Many times the pitcher, once he hears the warning, will step off and then run at the runner, who is then trapped in a rundown. Or, if he plays for a coordinated defense, the pitcher may jump pivot or use an "inside move" and then throw behind the runner to a middle infield coverman.

Like most things in baseball, stealing third base is part art and part science. And it takes a great sense of timing on the part of baserunners. They must have a good enough jump to beat the catcher's throw, but not take off so early that they tip the pitcher that they're on the move. In stealing second base, there is no similar worry, at least against right-handers. The runner basically challenges the defense. He is either going or he's not, and if he is, they have to react and throw him out. In stealing third, however, the runner may leave early enough to cause the defense to react before the ball is pitched.

Another difference in stealing third base is that there are two potential members of the defense who can take a throw at second base and tag the runner: the second baseman and the shortstop. At first and again at third base, the runner has only to worry about one coverman.

The runner at second is coached to watch the second baseman out of the corner of his eye, and to depend on the verbal signals from his third base coach to monitor movements of the shortstop. Some offenses will call "Step one" or "Back one," to communicate to the runner to take one more step toward third or to take one step back toward second, respectively, depending on what the middle infielders are doing. The runner who utilizes the walking lead off second has less of a view of the second baseman than the runner who leads off shuffle-style, which is another reason we liked the latter when leading from second base.

With the bases loaded and the pitcher working from a windup, the runner at second has to be particularly careful not to get picked off. A well-coordinated defense will have the pitcher toe the rubber in such a situation as if he is going to use a full windup, then disengage with the right foot and whirl and throw to a coverman at second. Because the bases are loaded, and because it "appears" that the opposing pitcher is working from a windup, the runner at second can be lulled into thinking that he needn't worry about a pickoff play behind him. Not to belabor the subject, but the runner is more vulnerable to this play when executing a walking lead. So again, we prefer the shuffle-style lead.

The runner at second is also vulnerable to the fake overthrow play in high school baseball. A couple of factors work in the favor of the defense here. First, there are two middle infielders and a centerfielder, three total defenders, available to "stage" the play, whereas you've only got one defender at first (unless you run it like Ron Frasier at Miami did it and get the bullpen and ballgirl involved) and one at third base on a hidden ball trick at those bases. The rules allow the pitcher to fake a throw from the rubber to second and third base, but not to first, so that comes into play as well. And there are base coaches at first and third to verbally instruct the runner not to get up and run when plays are attempted at those bases. So the runner at second is "on his own" when dealing with the fake overthrow.

The pitcher whirls and fakes a throw to second base and the runner dives back into the bag. One middle infielder stages "a miss," and dives for the ball as if it's gone through him. The other middle infielder yells, turns and sprints toward center field as if to recover an errant throw. And the centerfielder races in as if to scoop up the overthrow. With accompanying shouting and acceptable acting by the defenders, a jittery baserunner can be coaxed into at least jumping up and moving a few steps toward third base. Usually the second baseman will circle in behind him and be available for the rundown when the pitcher, who still has the ball, steps down off the mound and starts to trap the runner. I even saw one high school in Atlanta have their centerfielder drop a handkerchief in short center on the previous pitch, so that when the fake-overthrow play is executed on the next pitch, the runner would see a "flash of white" in centerfield that would resemble a baseball and be more inclined to jump up and edge toward third base. Personally, I found this action "over the top" and would not use it, even if helped get us an out. But that's just me.

So all in all, the runner at second base has a lot to think about. It's the only base where the runner is coached to execute two different primary leads, the 2-out semi-circle lead and the straight-line lead with nobody or one out. It's the only base where he has to contend with two juking defenders. And it's the only base where he has no base coach nearby in his ear to verbally assist and protect him. It is the "no man's land" for baserunners.

Now, back to stealing third. Assuming that third base is unoccupied, and that the runner on second is attempting the steal, he should watch the third baseman's position to see which corner of the bag he should slide to in order to avoid the tag. I'm not sure why, but you see more sliding injuries and tag related injuries at third base than at second. It may have something to do with the angle that the third baseman must take in order to take the throw and simultaneously apply a tag. A throw to the inside part of the bag can cause the third baseman to "kneel on" or "sit down on" the runner while applying the tag. Because of this, you'd like to see your runners going in feet first rather than head first, but we allowed our players to use their own judgment on sliding styles.

We once played a team who coached all their defensemen to crouch two to three feet from the bag, in the baseline, and take throws from the catcher while literally blocking the base. Early in the game we stole second, and our runner was jammed and tagged out, because the crouching defender would not allow him to get his feet all the way to second base. It's a dangerous and unsportsmanlike coaching technique. We had no choice but to coach our runners to "run right through" the crouching defenders enroute to the bag. One collision and the opposition stopped blocking the baselines and their fielders began taking throws from the catcher in normal fashion. You run into a lot of things coaching high school baseball, eh?

The catcher, once he has received the pitch and sees the runner attempting to take third base, must step up and throw in front of the hitter or step back and throw behind the hitter. The batter has the right to remain in his rightfully occupied position in the batter's box, so coach your right-handed hitters to take their stride and stay put on the steal of third. That is if they weren't swinging at the pitch. Coach them to avoid "guessing" with the catcher and trying to move out of his way. That territory is theirs. Just stay put and make the catcher work around them.

Leading Off Third

The last segment of this circular baserunning process occurs at third base. If you're working offense and defensive simultaneously, put a pitcher, catcher, and third baseman in their respective positions. Now, as your baserunner at third studies the field and is contacting the bag, he sees how far the third baseman is playing from the bag. This is essentially the distance that he can assume for the apex of his primary walking lead. Third base is the only base from which we coached our runners to utilize the walking lead.

As the pitcher receives his sign and begins his stretch, the runner should walk toward home. He should be facing home plate and his feet should be well outside the foul line. If the runner is hit by a batted ball in foul territory, he's okay; if he's hit in fair territory, he's out. It happens. So you want your runners taking their lead from third base in foul ground.

The runner wants to time his walking lead so that as the pitcher delivers, the runner is equally distant from the bag as the third baseman. The thinking, of course, is that the runner should be able to safely dive back to the bag,

*Figure 15. **Down in foul and back in fair.*** *Continue your walking lead and then your secondary lead in foul territory; then, when the pitch is handled cleanly at home plate, bust it back to the bag in fair territory.*

covering the same amount of ground that the third baseman would theoretically have to cover on an attempted pickoff play.

Have your pitcher, working from the stretch, throw the ball to the catcher four out of five times, but once every four or five pitches, have him practice his timing on the pickoff play with the third baseman. You don't want to do this too often, for the same reason that we don't practice the pickoff play to second "live" with runners very often. Too many potential injuries can occur. The ball can hit the runner. The runner can jam his fingers or hands diving back into the bag.

Now, let's say the pitcher goes home with the ball. The runner is walking toward home plate in foul territory. When the pitcher releases the baseball, the runner should take two skipping hops toward home that can propel him in that direction if the catcher doesn't handle the pitch cleanly and he makes an attempt to score on a passed ball or batted ball.

Have a coach stand in the left-hand side of the batter's box. The catcher practices catching and blocking every pitch. But once or twice every five or six pitches, the coach should toss a baseball toward the backstop (simulating a passed ball or wild pitch) just as the catcher catches the pitch. The runner then converts his "hop" toward home into a sprint toward the plate and runs through the plate standing up. He then jogs in foul territory around first, jogs to second, widens out into the short grass behind where the shortstop plays, and rejoins the line for the drill at third base.

Now, if the catcher handles the ball cleanly, and the coach makes no "passed ball or wild pitch" toss, the runner must "bust it back to the bag" at full speed. The runner should turn inward toward the infield, cross into fair territory, and sprint back to the bag. This takes away an easy sight and throwing lane for the catcher, who may want to make an attempt on the runner at third returning to the bag. "Down in foul, back in fair" is the mantra that you want to ingrain in your players early in the season.

Incorporate having your pitchers cover home and receiving a throw from the catcher on a wild pitch or passed ball while you're practicing walking leads at third, especially early in the season. You don't want any "plays at the plate," but have your runners sprint to the backstop side of home to avoid being hit by any throws. This way your pitchers and catchers can actually practice throwing to and covering home on the ball that gets away. Lot of high school ball games are won and lost on this play. How many times have you practiced it?

You can practice coordinating your catcher's "throw behind the runner" to third base between the catcher and the third baseman, and impart it into this drill. I recommend it. If an opposing baserunner is taking too big a lead or if he is lazy getting back, your catcher may be able to pick up an out throwing behind the runner after the pitch. Thus, you need to practice this. Again, injury is a possibility here, with balls hitting the runner and runners jamming fingers and hands diving back to the bag. But early season, you want to practice your leads at third base and your pickoffs and "throwbacks." Barring injury, any time you can simultaneously practice more than one aspect of the game, do it.

The other drill you should work on with your runners at third base involves reacting to a batted ball with less than two out. Put a runner on third base (keep your pitcher, catcher, and third baseman in their respective positions, fill the rest of the defensive positions, and have a coach at home plate hit fungoes) and have the runner react to various scenarios. The pitcher works from a windup and throws home, so the runner is executing his walking lead, and there is a line of batter-runners at home plate. When the ball reaches the plate, the coach calls out "Nobody out," and hits a long fly ball. The runner sprints back to the bag immediately to prepare to tag up. After the ball is caught, the runner races home. Then the coach calls "Nobody out," and hits a ground ball anywhere to the infield. With nobody out, our runners were coached to retreat to third base, or "make the ball go through," so the runner does just that while the infield makes the play on the live batter-runner.

Then the coach calls out, "One out," and hits a grounder at the shortstop. Our runners were coached to sprint home on any downward contact with one out, so the runner is off as soon as he sees the downward angle of the ball. If the shortstop makes the play at first, the batter-runner returns to the line at home plate. If the shortstop comes home with the ball, the runner runs behind home plate on the backstop side to avoid injury and collision, and the coach calls "Out" or "Safe" while the defense attempts to keep the trail runner from advancing to second base. Then, with the same call of "One out," have the coach hit a one-hopper right back to the pitcher. The runner, who is coached to sprint home on downward contact, sees the ball thrown home well in front of him, and reverses toward third. While the defense executes the rundown between third and home, the runner attempts to stay in the hotbox long enough to allow the batter-runner to advance to second. Meanwhile, the defense practices garnering the out between third and home without allowing the trail runner to advance to second base.

You see a lot of baserunning mistakes at third base in high school baseball. First, it's unfamiliar territory. Baserunners reach and occupy third less than the other two bases. Secondly, you are 90 feet away from that 17-inch slab, so attempting to advance from third to home means that a run is scored or not scored, which is the name of the game. So runners are nervous at third base. Thirdly, you are more likely to be hit by a batted ball at third base and make an out than at the other two bases, so it's the only base where you take your lead in foul territory. And, if it's not a force play, being a runner at third presents the special challenge of knowing whether to move on downward contact, "read" the ball, or sit tight and make the ball go through before you move.

Tagging up on fly balls and attempting to advance occurs most often at third base. Here's a simple baserunning rule, one that must be emphasized and drilled and coached daily: With less than two outs, on fly balls to the outfield, you must return to the bag immediately on a fly ball, because you're normally going to score whether the outfielder catches the ball or not.

What's the big deal here? Well, it's natural for a baserunner to make an instinctive move toward the next base on a batted ball of any kind. On a fly ball to the outfield with less than two outs, though, your runner must be continually coached that there is only one movement he must make: *back to the bag immediately*. If the ball is caught in the outfield, the runner will already be back at the bag and in tag up position, ready to sprint for home. If the ball is not caught, he will score anyway a vast majority of the time, even having come back to the bag. So there is no disadvantage in retreating to third immediately on a fly ball with less than two down.

But very frequently you will see baserunners move forward two or three steps toward home while the fly ball is in the air. Then, it will dawn on them that the ball might be caught, and that they should retreat and tag up. Very often the baserunner is still retreating to the bag as the outfielder makes the catch, and the outfielder hits the cutoff man and the runner is just now starting his movement home after tagging up, and he doesn't score or attempt to score.

You see this baserunning error at the college level and even sometimes at the major league level. You see it quite often at the high school level. And I cannot emphasize this enough. Baserunning mistakes are rally killers, and if you get a baserunner to third, it is vital that you communicate and coach effectively in practice and in games to give that runner the best chance to score.

STEALING HOME

High school teams do not practice stealing home very often, but like the delayed steal, it's definitely a bullet you want to be able to fire when the situation calls for it. And when is that?

Well, we liked to attempt to steal home if we had excellent speed and baserunning skill at third; if the pitcher was working from a windup and had a slow delivery; if the pitcher frequently missed with breaking pitches in the dirt; if the pitcher generally employed a lot of off-speed pitches; and if there were two out and the chances of scoring the runner were better with the steal than with waiting on a base hit from the hitter.

The distance that the third baseman played off the bag was a factor as well, though if the pitcher was working from the windup this was usually less of a concern. Most high school pitchers do not have a good step off and throw to third move from the windup position. Some do, but it's rare. So a runner can usually assume an excellent primary lead at third base against a pitcher working from the windup.

It sounds implausible, but a good technique paired with good speed can make it a fairly easy offensive maneuver. I found this out the hard way early in my career. I inherited a 6'7" string bean of a pitcher. His first love was basketball, but every year about six games into our season (basketball and baseball seasons overlapped in California) he would come up and get his arm in shape and by mid-season, he would assume a spot in our rotation. He had better than average stuff, and his height and arm angle gave hitters problems.

Late spring, he's won four or five games in a row and is on the hill in the league championship tournament semi-finals. Game is tied 3-3 in the bottom of the sixth and our opponent has a runner at third with two out. We're working from the windup, because we're focusing on retiring the hitter, not the baserunner, with two down. Well, our big guy gets the sign, collects himself, and slowly goes into his rock step. Meanwhile, their runner on third has taken off and is tearing down the line. Our guy's delivery was so slow that their baserunner could have gone in standing up. I think he slid into the plate to avoid possibly getting hit by the pitch. But it wasn't even close.

They hold us without scoring in the top of the seventh and bing-bang-boom, the steal of home knocks us out of the league tournament. That taught me something. From then on, we practiced stealing home, and practiced with our pitchers on defending the steal of home.

Timing is everything on the steal of the home. With a pitcher on the mound working from the windup and throwing to a live catcher and a third baseman holding, have your team line up at third base, with a hitter in the box. You practice stealing home in groups of three, using two throwdown bases extended in foul territory adjacent to the third base bag. The players practice receiving their sign on the bag, while the hitter, stepping out with one foot from the right side, gets his "steal of home and take" sign.

The players assume their primary lead while watching the pitcher. You move down the line, turn toward the third baseman and serve to warn the runner if the third baseman is making a move to set up for a pickoff throw. Call "You're okay," or "Back one" to move the runner down the line or back toward third, or "BACK" as loud as you can if the pickoff attempt is on.

Physically, you are standing between the first and second runners, but are watching and verbally communicating only with the "live" runner moving down the actual baseline. The other two "dummy" runners, however, move back and forth and back to the bag on your command to the "live" runner.

*Figure 16. **Practicing the steal of home.** Gauge your primary lead based on how far from the bag the third baseman is playing. Get a walking lead, facing home plate directly, and when the pitcher begins his motion, get your guts up and get gone. In this drill, the "outside runner" advancing from the throwdown base may have a chance.*

The players have assumed their primary leads. The third baseman is not a threat. And the pitcher toes the rubber. Just before the pitcher begins his windup, the baserunners execute a short walking lead, enough to give them a huge jump but hopefully not enough to entice a pickoff throw or step off by the pitcher. Now the pitcher begins his windup. You give the command "Go!," and the three baserunners convert their walking lead into a full-speed sprint. The outside two baserunners sprint straight through the area behind the catcher. And the "live" runner, upon the "Go!" command, veers behind the second "dummy" runner to also pass behind the catcher and avoid injury from being hit by the pitch or colliding with the catcher. The batter holds his ground and then as the pitch nears, steps toward third base with his front foot, giving the baserunner a big part of the plate to slide to.

The coaching corollary to this "runner at third on a fly ball with less than two out" conundrum is: How does the runner at third react on a ground ball with less than two out?

I have seen this situation coached differently in different programs. Here's how we coached our runners at third base:

With nobody out and no trail runner, the runner at third must make a ground ball go through the infield before he starts for home. We are "playing it safe" on all passed balls, wild pitches, and batted balls with no one out. We feel like the chances are excellent that you can score later in the inning, so take no unnecessary chances with nobody out.

With nobody out and a trail runner, the runner at third is racing for home on "downward contact," regardless of where the ball is hit. If the throw beats him home, he must engage the catcher in a rundown and stay in it as long as possible to allow the trail runner to advance.

With one out, the runner at third is racing for home on "downward contact," regardless of where the ball is hit. If the throw beats him home, he must engage the catcher in a rundown and stay in it as long as possible to allow a trail runner and or batter/runner to advance.

With two outs, the runner at third is racing for home on any batted ball, regardless of the angle of the ball off the bat.

Now, many coaches, and some of you, no doubt, will differ with our philosophy of always sending the runner from third on downward contact with one out. What if the ball is hit right back to the pitcher and the runner races into an out at home plate? Or what if it's a line drive one-hopper to the third baseman, who can make an easy throw to the catcher to nail your runner?

Well, this certainly can and does happen. And as you have read, if it does, the runner's job is to initiate a rundown and stay in it as long as possible, allowing the trail runner to advance. But you are right. Sometimes you'll give up an easy out doing this.

*Figure 17. **Runner in a rundown between third and home**. If you're on third with one out, we're sending you full speed on all downward contact. If you're on third with nobody out and a trail runner aboard, we're still going on downward contact. That's our philosophy, pressure the defense to make a play. Knowing you're going to try to take home on any downward contact maximizes your jump and can mean the difference between scoring and not scoring on a bang-bang play at the plate. Now, if it's a one-hopper back to the pitcher and the catcher is waiting on you with the ball at home plate 20 feet before you arrive, your job is to stay in the "hotbox" as long as you can. Maybe they'll botch the rundown and maybe they won't, but at the very least, stay in it long enough for the trail runners or batter-runner to advance as far as possible. With nobody out and no trail runner, we'll probably "make it go through" before sending you.*

Here's our thinking. First, we want to avoid any baserunning mistakes created by indecision. If a kid has to watch the ball and make a decision on his own whether to attempt to score or not, many times the opportunity to initiate his run to the plate has been lost by the time he starts toward home. In coaching, it's always preferable to give a kid a rule to play by, rather than asking him to make a decision, under pressure, on the fly.

Secondly, this aggressive philosophy pressures the defense. If the shortstop sees we're going on downward contact every time we get a runner to third, he knows he's got to make a clean play and a good throw. The opposition may also bring the defense "in," one step off the grass, to combat our aggressive style at third. Well, this makes it harder to score on ground balls, but it opens up great hitting angles. As they say, when the infield is in, it turns a .250 hitter into a .400 hitter. Which is another reason that we emphasize hard downward contact in our hitting drills. Hard ground balls and line drives will score you runs in high school baseball.

⚾ ⚾ ⚾

Here's another baserunning-rules occurrence worth discussing with your team on a rainy day. We're playing our cross-town rival in Texas, and they're an aggressive baserunning team. Top of the first inning they've got runners on first and third and nobody out and their no. 3 hitter rips a one-hopper to our third baseman.

Well, the trail runner was running on the pitch, so our third baseman has no chance to go to second to start the 5-4-3 double play. And their lead runner at third was off with the downward contact, so our third baseman throws home to cut the run. The catcher receives the ball well ahead of the runner's arrival, so a rundown ensues. Their lead runner is doing just what he's supposed to do, staying alive in the rundown, which gives the trail runner time to advance as far as he can.

And the trail runner makes it all the way to third. Their lead runner dances and jukes and somehow avoids a tag, but decides to retreat to third when we fail to tag him out in the rundown. Now the opposition has two players standing on third base.

Well, our catcher, who ran the lead runner all the way back to third, does just what he's been taught, and tags both runners with his mitt with the ball in it. The rule, of course, is that the lead runner has the right to the bag, so technically, our catcher only needed to tag the trail runner in order to get the available out. But I always told our kids, "They screw up and get two guys on base, tag 'em both. Don't worry about which one rightfully occupies the bag. Just tag 'em both. The umpire will figure out the play afterwards. There's no rule against tagging a player who is legally occupying a base." I just didn't want our defensive players having to think about interpreting a rule in the heat of battle. So our defensive mantra was "Tag 'em both."

Well, as soon as our catcher tagged both runners, the nearest umpire threw his fist in the air and yelled, "The trail runner is out!" And the trail runner continued to stand uneasily on the bag. But for some reason, the lead runner got spooked when the ump yelled, and he took off for home plate, thinking that he must vacate the bag. Thankfully, our pitcher had covered home during the rundown and was still standing near the plate. So all our catcher had to do was move outside the foul line and throw a dart to our pitcher at home plate to beat the lead runner heading home. He tried to score standing up and we got him out easily.

So now we had a double play and there were two out. The batter runner stopped at second base and we got the next guy to pop up—the inning and the scoring threat were over. We go on to win 3-0, and there's no doubt that that one play turned the game around.

So you see, baserunning and rules instruction go hand-in-hand. Their lead runner did just what he was supposed to do. With nobody out and a trail runner aboard, head home on downward contact. If the ball beats you there by a considerable margin, initiate a rundown and stay alive in it as long as you can. What he didn't anticipate was that the trail runner would join him at third base when he retreated there. And then when the ump yelled "The trail runner is out," he didn't realize that he legally occupied the bag, and could simply stay put. Had he done that, the opposition would have had second and third with one out with their cleanup hitter at the plate, and would have probably scored and changed the tenor and maybe the outcome of the game.

It pays to "talk baseball" with your players. You can do it in a relaxed, bull session type of format in the locker room prior to practice, during rain delays in summer ball, anytime you and your guys are spending time together. To get the conversation started, ask one of your veterans, "Hey Andy, remember that game when Oak Hill got two players trapped on third?" Your veteran will laugh and say, "Yeah," and invariably, another player will ask what happened. Well that opens the door to storytelling, as opposed to a lecture on baseball rules, and then you can bring up other occurrences that your kids can relate to that illuminate rules for them in a relaxed atmosphere.

Why do I harp on this? Ever watch runners react in a high school game when an ump calls the infield fly rule? It's the American athletic high school version of musical chairs. Nobody, and I mean nobody, truly understands the infield fly rule. Don't believe me? Ask one of your players what it means.

There are two problems with the infield fly rule. One, players are asked to interpret a rule on their own, while action is occurring on the field. And two, it is one of the few times the umpire will actually yell on the field to communicate to players, and that scares high school players into making mistakes. You know the drill. Runners on first and second and nobody out. Your hitter hits a lazy pop up on the grass just behind second base. The middle infielders are running over and about to call "Ball!," meaning "I've got it," and the ump hollers, "Infield fly rule! The batter is out!"

And then what happens? The runners are frozen like deer in the headlights, right? They don't know what to do. Half the time the middle infielders will become discombobulated and confused as well and let the ball drop in between them. This further confounds the runners, who think now that they must advance to the next base in order to avoid a force out.

As you know, as soon as the ump calls "Infield fly rule," the batter can retreat to the dugout, because he is out, and the runners can return to their previously occupied bases, because they advance "at their own risk," and they would not normally attempt to advance, or tag up and take the next base, on a shallow pop up. But half the time the ball isn't caught, and this confuses everyone. And even if a fielder makes the play, runners are frequently trapped off base, thinking that they must do something different than just play baseball.

Truthfully, I'm not sure that the infield fly rule serves much purpose in high school baseball. The rule's intent, as far as I can tell, is to prevent a fielder from purposely dropping a routine fly in order to create a force play (or, a double- or triple-play) and take unfair advantage of runners who may assume that the ball will be caught and will naturally stay close to their previously occupied base. If the infield fly rule were removed from the high school rulebook, how many times would you actually see a defensive team purposely letting a pop fly fall to the ground? In my opinion, you could play a season's worth of games before you saw a kid purposely drop a routine pop up to try to create a double play. Anyway, back to coaching baserunners.

We always coached our players this way: If you hear the umpire call "infield fly rule," runners should return to their previous base and batter-runners should return to the dugout. That's all they need to know. But it's amazing how many times jittery baserunners take off and get themselves tagged out when they hear the ump make that call. Just emphasize to your runners and batter-runner: Go back where you came from. That's it.

Many umpires are, I must say, excited to make this call. It shows that they know the rules. If I was in their shoes, I probably would be fired up about making the call as well. But instead of helping the game, this verbal call by the ump seems to disturb the game. Mention eliminating the infield fly rule at your next state rules meeting and see what happens. Maybe you can get it removed, or start a dialogue to take it out of the game.

Umpires can play a huge role in the outcome of ballgames. Fortunately, most are very professional and give their best effort each time out, and thus let the players decide the game's outcome. But here's an example of an umpire failing to initiate a signal and verbal call that cost us dearly. We've got first and second and nobody out in the first round of a big, big tournament game. It's the top of the first and we're really cooking offensively, even though the opposition is top notch. Our no. 3 hitter comes up and smokes a stream of milk to left center. I mean he really blisters it.

Their centerfielder comes flying in to make a play on the ball and it's unclear whether he'll even be able to get to it, much less make a play on it. So both of our baserunners are doing that "ants in the pants" dance, where they're marking time, waiting to sprint for the next base, but with nobody out, not wanting to get doubled off should the outfielder make a stupendous play.

Well, wouldn't you know it, the kid in centerfield makes the play of the year just to get his glove near the ball. When it was first hit, I didn't think their kid could get anywhere near it. But he came hard and fast and he was a left-handed thrower, so he had the glove on his right hand, closest to the side that the ball was hit. Anyway, he's sprinting in toward left center at full speed, our baserunners are turned watching and waiting, and the outfielder reaches down at the last second and stabs at the ball. His glove sort of smothers the ball and snowcones it and he comes head over heels and turns a couple of somersaults with the ball appearing to bounce around somewhere on his body.

Everybody in the ballpark is staring at the field ump, waiting for a call. And the field ump just stands there like a spectator. I mean, we've got to have a call. Even if he gets it wrong, you can't not make a call and leave the baserunners stranded and the defense flummoxed and everybody in confusion. I mean, make a call, for cryin' out loud.

Well, to make matters worse, the field ump never moved toward the play, never exhibited the slightest effort to get closer to the spot where the fielder intersected the flight of the ball to get a better vantage point. In fact, he never even turned his whole body around toward center field. He just kept his hands on his knees and turned his head toward center.

Meanwhile, the whole ballpark is suspended in time. The kid in center is still rolling around and the ball is flashing white somewhere under his body in the confusion. Did he catch it? Did he trap it? Is he holding the ball against his body? Do we have a catch or not?

Now I'm in a no-win spot in the third base coaching box. You understand my dilemma. Finally, after what seemed like an eternity, I gave up waiting. Maybe this ump's signal for a "no catch" is no signal at all, I think. I don't know. All I know is, our baserunners have got to move one way or the other. So I yell and wave them on and they comply, with our lead runner pounding toward me at third and getting set to round the sack and push off for home. I'm waving him around third base, looking at the kid in center to time the throw versus our baserunners, when I see the field ump slowly raise his arm and signal "Catch."

The whole ballpark just erupted. Somehow I got our lead runner turned around and headed back toward second base. The trail runner saw everything in front of him and began retreating sooner. The centerfielder, after he finally recovered the ball and found his footing, made a decent throw to second and doubled off our lead runner. The second baseman took the throw and turned and threw to first in an attempt to complete the trifecta. But our trail runner slid back in to beat the throw and avoid a triple play.

The defense was literally hysterical with joy. Our fans were extremely unhappy, as were our players. The field ump just froze and never made a call until it was too late. By the time he finally raised his hand to signal an out, the kids had basically begun playing the game without him.

I don't think the centerfielder actually caught the ball. I think he trapped it on a short hop and then cradled the ball to his body as he somersaulted. Then he showed the ball in his throwing hand coming out of his dive. Well, it was a heck of a play on his part and I give him credit. What I couldn't abide was the field umpire making no effort to see the play more clearly by moving toward the spot, then simply standing like a statue while the ballgame continued around him.

I went out and argued. I never argued whether the ball was caught or not. That to me was immaterial. What was relevant was the fact that our baserunners were placed in an impossible position by the umpire's failure to make a call. Any call. This kind of thing, fortunately, is rare, but it happens. You get bad calls at the college and pro level, but at that level you are less likely to get a "no call" from a field umpire who doesn't move toward the play to get a closer look. It's one of the many challenges of coaching high school baseball, right?

We go from first and second and nobody out, with our no. 3 hitter up, to two outs and a runner on first. We fail to score that inning and it really changed the game's momentum. We went on to win, but that call gave the opposition new life in a game where we had started very sharply.

Fortunately, most umps are hustlers and give you their best effort, so this kind of sloppy performance is rare. But it happens sometimes. And you've got to learn to deal with it. Today I can laugh telling the story. That day I was staring daggers at the field ump for the rest of the day.

One final note. I guess I made a real enemy the day I went out and argued that call, because the field ump who stood like a statue and refused to signal "Catch" or "No Catch" harbored a grudge. I know this because I ran into him at the golf course about a year later. He's working as a starter on the back nine, and I'm teeing off with my son.

And I'm friendly to him. It's all in the past to me now. But I can tell he's still got a burr up his behind. So just to pass the time while we're waiting to hit, I say, "Jack, whatcha' been doing lately? I haven't seen you calling any games." And without missing a beat, he says, right in front of my son, "I stopped calling games. Too many asshole coaches." Well, what could I do. So I teed my ball up and turned to him and said, "You know, Jack, you may be right. But it's been my experience that the number of asshole coaches is exactly equal to the number incompetent, lazy umpires." And then we hit and walked away from him. Some fences can't be mended.

First and Third Versus a Lefty Play

With runners on first and third and a left-handed pitcher on the mound, you have the opportunity to attempt to steal a run if you choose. A quick summary of the play's strategy is this: The runner on first takes a larger than normal lead and intentionally draws a throw to first base, while the runner on third takes off for home. We'll discuss the fine points in a moment.

We always preferred to run this play with two outs, which is somewhat akin to waving a runner from second base and trying to score him on a base hit. With nobody out, you have a good chance to score your lead runner later in the inning anyway, so why bust up a potential big inning. But with two outs, and in some cases with one out, it can be a good gamble. If you have a lefty hitting, and he struggles against lefty pitching, this is a good time to put the play on. If your base runner on third has some speed, this helps, also. Or, if you're down in the lineup with two down and you simply think that you have a better chance of scoring with this base running play than you do of waiting for a base hit, go ahead and put the play on. If you're battering the opposing lefty, forget this play and swing the bat. But if he's giving you trouble, here's a play that will allow you to score on him.

Will it work? In a word, yes. Earl Weaver used to run this play with the Baltimore Orioles and it rarely failed. We probably only used this play half a dozen times a season, but here is the thing: in all my years of coaching high school baseball, we never failed to score on this play if we were able to entice the pitcher to throw over. Many times the first baseman will throw the ball away attempting to nail the lead runner, and the trail runner will advance to third base on the play. If you really want to play small ball, execute the play with one out, score the lead runner and advance the trail runner to third, and call for the squeeze on the next pitch while the defense is still reeling from their mistake. So you score twice with a left-handed hitter facing a left-handed pitcher. That's pretty good baseball.

You must coach and practice this play two to three times a week in pre-season and once a week in-season to keep your players familiar with the tactics. Here's how it works. You have runners on first and third and you're facing a left-handed pitcher. Your trail runner at first base takes one extra sideways step on his primary lead. Coach the trail runner to take just enough extra lead so that the pitcher will be enticed to throw over to attempt to pick him off, but not so much of a lead that the pitcher will want to step off the rubber or step off and run toward the runner. Just tell your trail runners in practice drills to assume their normal 12-foot, 4-step lead, then to take one more large, side to side step, which will place him about 15 feet from the bag at first. That's a big lead and it's virtually impossible for a lefty to ignore.

The pitcher knows there's a lead runner behind him at third base, but he sees the trail runner and thinks, "Hey, I can pick this guy off." It's almost impossible for the pitcher to go home with the ball in this situation. The opportunity to record an easy out on the pickoff is just too inviting. So he steps toward first base and throws over on the attempted pickoff.

Two things must happen when the pitcher lifts his stride leg, and both are crucial to the play's success. First, the lead runner at third must break for home immediately. Not when he sees that the pitcher is actually going to first with the ball, but as soon as the pitcher lifts his stride leg. If by some small chance the pitcher lifts his stride leg and goes home with the ball, the lead runner at third will see this, and even though he's in a full sprint toward home, he'll be able to turn back inside into fair territory and haul it back to the bag in time to beat a throw from the catcher. But trust me, if the trail runner at first executes the play correctly, the pitcher will be stepping toward and throwing to first. But it's absolutely vital that the lead runner at third take off for home as soon as the pitcher lift his stride leg.

With the pitcher lifting his stride leg and the lead runner at third base breaking for home, the trail runner at first must freeze momentarily, as if he's been caught napping. Then when the pitcher actually releases the baseball toward first, the runner should take two steps back toward the bag, as if he's going to try to return safely to first. The trail runner at first wants the first baseman to catch the pitcher's pickoff attempt well before he nears the bag. But he wants to be close enough to the first baseman so that the first baseman sees the opportunity of an out within a few feet. Once the first baseman has the baseball, and he feels and sees the runner trying to come back to first, he'll hold the ball momentarily. Then, when the first baseman receives the pickoff throw, the runner will reverse direction and light out full speed for second base.

Meanwhile, the lead runner at third has been pounding for home. The opposing dugout will see the play unfold, and oftentimes they'll begin hollering "Home, home!" to the first baseman as soon as he catches the ball. But rarely will the first baseman move out toward the pitcher, accept the pickoff throw and then release a throw toward home immediately. Instead, he'll invariably dicker with the runner at first momentarily. Then, the realization that a run is about to score will hit him suddenly, and 9 times out of 10 he'll attempt a rushed throw to home. Your lead runner will score, trust me. And your trail runner should be coached to sprint full speed for second base and make the turn and look for the opportunity to take third on a bad throw from the first baseman that gets by the catcher. Worst case scenario, your trail runner will be in scoring position at second.

But as I mentioned, if you execute the play with one out and actually advance the trail runner to third on the play, putting on the suicide squeeze on the next pitch is an excellent small ball move. We never liked the suicide squeeze that much, because if your hitter misses the bunt, it's tantamount to giving the defense an out. But we did like it in this situation. The bunt always works best as a surprise and when the defense has just made a mistake. The defense will be on their heels in the wake of this first and third play and is often unprepared to deal with the squeeze play on the next pitch. Many times you'll get a bad throw to first base from the third baseman, especially if he's been caught napping and has to rush in to play the bunt, and you'll get your batter/bunter to second base on the play and have another runner in scoring position.

Early in pre-season, put this play on in an intra-squad game and keep the defense in the dark about the play. This will allow you to see a "live" version of how a typical high school pitcher and defense will react to the play. You don't want to take the bat out of your hitters' hands too often, but if this is your best chance to score, take it. It'll work.

First and Second Jam Up Play

You start this play during your opponent's pre-game infield drill by watching the first baseman. Can he throw it across the diamond accurately in pre-game? Is he a younger player, possibly prone to rushing a throw under pressure? Either way, here's how you again take advantage of the first baseman on a specialty play.

You run the "Jam Up" play with runners on first and second. You can call for it against a righty or a lefty. Basically, you send the trail runner on a straight steal as the pitcher goes home. About halfway down, he "realizes" that the base in front of him is occupied, and "attempts" to sprint back to first base. You entice the catcher to throw to first base behind the trail runner, and the instant that the catcher releases the ball to first, both runners light out for the next base. This forces the first baseman to throw, often to a moving target, across the diamond to third base to attempt to get the lead runner. We'll detail it out in a moment.

Unlike the first and third play, we like to put the "Jam Up" play on most often with nobody out and a fresh count on the hitter. I like this play in lieu of a sacrifice bunt, which many high school teams will call for in this situation. It's the old "bunt in order" situation, right? First and second and nobody out. But instead of giving up an out with the sac bunt, you force the defense to make a couple of split-second decisions and challenging throws and never have to give up the out at the plate. Here's how it works.

Both runners take their normal primary leads. When the pitcher goes home with the ball, your trail runner is off with the pitch on a straight steal of second base. The hitter takes the pitch. When the ball reaches home plate, and the trail runner is about halfway to second, the coach and the "bench" begin hollering "Back! Back!" to the trail runner, who stops in his tracks and "pretends" to begin a sprint back toward first base.

The catcher receives the pitch, sees the trail runner "trapped" and trying to return to first, and thinks, "I've got this sucker now," and he comes up out of his crouch and fires a throw to the first baseman, who has moved to the bag to receive the throw. Couple of things here. The lead runner moves from his primary to his secondary lead as the pitcher releases the ball, then he waits for the catcher to commit to first base before he sprints for third. Unlike the first and third vs. a lefty play, where the lead runner must commit and sprint for home the instant that the pitcher lifts his stride leg, the lead runner at second on this play must wait and make sure that the catcher actually releases the baseball toward first base. If he breaks too soon, the catcher will be tipped off and will turn his attention to the lead runner and attempt to make a play on him instead. Sometimes, too, a veteran catcher will pump fake to first as if he's making a play on the trail runner, and will hope to catch the lead runner taking off for third and then trap him in a rundown. Not many high school catchers will think this fast, but it happens. So the lead runner has got to wait until the catcher actually releases the throw to first base before he takes off for third. He'll make it anyway, 9 times out of 10.

The trail runner must also delay his reversal of direction back toward second until the catcher actually releases the baseball toward first base. This is to avoid having the catcher "run at him" or pump fake. We want the catcher to see a trapped runner retreating to first base, a runner that represents an easy out. Then, when the catcher actually releases the ball to first, the lead runner takes off for third and the trail runner reserves direction and sprints full speed for second base.

Now once the catcher has released the ball, the play turns in your favor. First, the catcher is throwing to a first baseman unexpectedly, one who has not been holding the runner (most teams don't hold the trail runner with runners at first and second, right?), and the first baseman is a moving target, sprinting from his defensive spot to the bag to receive the catcher's throw. The catcher has been thinking about defensing the bunt on the "bunt in order" play, and suddenly he's required to hit the first baseman with a throw on demand. Certainly a doable task, but nothing's for certain in high school baseball.

Now, assume that the catcher makes a good throw to the first baseman and that the first baseman gloves the ball cleanly. Which will probably happen. The first baseman moved to the bag expecting to receive a throw and slap a tag down on the trail runner, right? Well, he receives the throw, looks up, and suddenly both runners are moving toward the next bag. So he's got to try to get the lead runner. Nineteen times out of 20, the first baseman will throw across the diamond to third in an attempt to nab the lead runner.

Well, the third baseman hardly ever is required to make this throw in a game. When was the last game situation when your first baseman threw the ball to third base? On a bunt? How many times has your third baseman come charging in and grabbed a bunt and made the decision to throw to third base to get the lead runner there? It just hardly ever happens in high school baseball. There aren't many Keith Hernandez's out there. Hernandez may have been the greatest in the history of baseball at defensing the bunt from his position at first base.

What will happen most often is this. The first baseman will receive the catcher's throw and realize that he's got to throw to third base to get the lead runner, who has just broken for third. And he's oftentimes got to hit a moving target over there. The third baseman's not at the bag, see? He's been playing either even with the bag, at double play depth, or possibly in on the grass to defense the bunt in order play, right? Either way, the third baseman is caught by surprise as well, and he's got to sprint to the bag and await the third baseman's throw.

So the first baseman is throwing to a moving target, all the way across the diamond, in a sudden, "on demand" situation, and is asked to make a throw he may make once all season. The odds are all in your favor. Seven times out of 10, the throw will be off line, will bounce and handcuff the third baseman, or will sail wide or over his head, so that the play will not even be close. Frequently, the lead runner can execute a pop-up slide and sprint on home as the ball rattles down into foul territory beyond third base. An experienced, talented first baseman may nail your lead runner here, but that's why you watch pre-game infield. And you call for this play against a first baseman who might still be a little "green". We ran this play, like the first and third play, maybe only a half dozen times a season, but it rarely failed.

Be prepared to wave your lead runner home on a bad throw, or keep him at the bag if the third baseman did a good job blocking a bad throw from the first baseman. But be prepared to make visual contact with the trail runner immediately thereafter (if you waved the lead runner home) and see if you can get him to third base on the play. Both your runners should be coached to look for the extra base if a bad throw occurred, which it often will.

Once in a blue moon the catcher will simply hold the ball, having been coached "never to throw behind a runner, or especially a trail runner." In that case, the trail runner simply returns to first, and you've still got first and second and nobody out. It's awful tempting, though, for the catcher to want to showcase his arm and nail a "dead duck" who made a third grade base running mistake, and a huge majority of the time the catcher will throw to first and put the play in motion for you.

CHAPTER TWELVE
HAVE IT YOUR WAY

"But it's alright now . . . I learned my lesson well . . .
You see you can't please everyone . . . so you got to please yourself."

Garden Party as performed by Ricky Nelson

Ad executives at Burger King concocted a very appealing campaign years back with the catchy phrase, "Have it your way," meaning that you could order your hamburger with or without onions, pickles, and the like, and in the process get exactly the kind of hamburger you wanted. That's essentially what you've got to do in coaching high school baseball: Find out what kind of offensive philosophy you want to employ by figuring out what works for you, then try and make it happen, regardless of what others think. Try to make your team play your way.

If you embrace our aggressive offensive philosophy, you're going to run into some outs. There's just no way around it. And sometimes you'll look bad, even dumb. Over the course of a season, though, and certainly over the course of your coaching career, I think you'll score far many more runs by putting the pedal to the medal.

Whatever your offensive philosophy, make it your own and live by it. I think it was Shakespeare who said, "To thine own self be true." Win or lose with your own methods, not by someone else's.

Here's the rub. Most folks aren't going to like you anyway, so you might as well coach the way you want to. It's a sad fact that you can't be a really successful coach and be everyone's best friend. The two are simply not compatible. You've got to cut kids and put kids on the bench and discipline kids and sometimes kick them off the team. It's not always pleasant. So if you really care what people think about you, it's probably not the right profession for you. As President Harry Truman is alleged to have said, "If you want a friend in this life, get a dog." Don't get me wrong, you can still be a good person. It's just that people may not like your decisions.

Here's an example. As I mentioned, I'm in business with my family now. And as part of my duties, I attend a meeting of a homeowner's association. And there at the meeting is a 40ish executive in shirt and tie who looks familiar. After the meeting I approach him and shake hands and say, "You sure look familiar." And he smiles and says, "Hi Coach, Tommy Nabors. You cut me from the baseball team my senior year."

Now, understand, he wasn't being unfriendly, and we chatted for a moment after that. But that was the first thing out of his mouth when he saw me. It was a part of his high school experience that he would always remember whenever he thought of me. And that's not something you want for yourself.

The fact that he didn't deserve to make the team was irrelevant. He was a shot-putter, a track man, who had never played high school baseball, or even played any kind of baseball as far as I knew. His best friend was our starting shortstop, and I think he wanted spend the spring of his senior year traveling with his buddy on our ball club.

Well, no. 1, if I kept him, he wasn't ever going to play. And one of the first rules of coaching high school baseball is if you are going to keep a senior, you'd better play him, because he's going to be an unhappy camper sitting behind an underclassman, and that's a recipe for trouble. And no. 2, you've only got 18 uniforms. If you keep him, you've got to cut someone else. Now, is that fair to the other kid who gets cut?

But none of that mattered to Tommy. The only thing he knew was that I had cut him from the team during his senior year of high school.

I mentioned earlier about a player who was crushed when I benched him in favor of a kid who had just joined us from basketball, and how I lost an assistant coach over my actions. That was ugly and unfortunate. But from my point of view, it was unavoidable. I had no choice but to do what I did.

Here's the deal. In Georgia, basketball season and baseball season overlap, and we'd usually play about six or seven games before hoops ended and any basketball players who played baseball joined us. Our starting first baseman was a basketballer, a 6'6" kid who could hit for power and who could really pick it at first base. Not the kind of kid you could afford to leave on the bench.

So, basketball season ends, and Jack, our big first baseman joins us, and we play a game two days later. And I stick him out there. Problem is, somebody that's been playing has got to go to the bench, right? So I move the guy who had been starting at first to right field, and I put our right fielder temporarily on the bench. Now the right fielder who got benched had started the first six games of the year, and he played reasonably well. Hadn't knocked down any fences, but he had contributed. But when Jack joined us, somebody had to sit down, and our right fielder was our weakest link.

Well, first game after basketball season, we're playing on the road, and Jack's out there at first base like he's been there with us all season. He smashes two doubles and hits a single and makes all the plays at first base, including some very difficult pickups. I mean it's obvious the kid belongs out there. He doesn't even need a few games to get his timing back. He's that good a player. And helps us win a big game.

But our right fielder is devastated, and he confides in one of our assistant coaches, who comes to me the next day after practice and says, "Tim is really hurting that you benched him. It's not fair. He shouldn't have to sit because Jack came out from basketball."

Well, I'm trying to win games. I'm charged with putting the best team on the field I can, every day, with what I've got to work with. And sometimes guys get their feelings hurt when you do that. It's inevitable. But our assistant coach, a good guy who was volunteering his time, just couldn't understand it. And he says, "Well, if Tim has to sit, then I'm quitting." What could I say? I thanked him for his time and for working with the kids and said sorry, but that's the way it's got to be.

You see, you can't please everyone. There's only so many spots out there. And not everybody can play every game. Now, should I have handled it differently with Tim? Should I have gone to him and talked to him about why I was sitting him down? Maybe. But what could I have said that would have made him feel better? "Tim, Jack's out from basketball now and he's better than you and so is everybody else that's starting, so you've got to sit down until we need you?" That's the truth, but should I have told him that? I don't know.

I sure didn't want to lose a valued assistant coach. He was a good man and an excellent assistant. But you have to win games, not popularity contests. Making these kinds of difficult decisions is one of the things I miss least about coaching.

> "Eat everybody while you can, because the next young fuzzy-ball shark-trained from adolescence just to defeat your style of game- will come soon enough . . . despite their different ages, Borg, Ali and Nicklaus must all operate on the same assumption: Don't save anything for tomorrow, since there may not be one."
>
> Thomas Bowell in *Strokes of Genius*

It's tough sometimes. My Dad's hunting buddy played some professional baseball. When he heard I was going into high school coaching, he called me aside one day and said, "Kenny, I just want to tell you one thing. When you're out there on that field, you beat their butts. Worry about everything else later. But when you're on that field, you beat their butts."

I just grinned and said, "Sure." What could I say? He was an older man who meant well. I mean, what else was I going to try to do but win?

Well, my second year in Texas we've got a pretty decent ball club. We had improved markedly through our summer and fall ball schedules and gotten significantly stronger in our off-season weight program. And down the stretch in league play, we had won five or six in a row and we're starting to make some noise.

We go play our cross-town rival and we jump all over their starter in the first two innings and take an 11-0 lead. I mean we're cruising. So I pull everybody but our starting pitcher. Great opportunity for our backups to get some playing time in a league game, right?

Well, our reserves make every conceivable error in the field and we can't buy a base hit, and by the sixth inning our opponent has whittled our lead down to 11-8. So I throw our starters back in there (Texas has the one-time substitute and return rule, like most states), but by now, it's too late. We've lost the momentum. The game goes into extra innings and we end up losing 13-12.

The grief I took over that loss is difficult to describe. I mean I got blasted from all corners. Our parents were really angry at me. Bad coaching, bad decisions, what was he thinking? Even our local newspaper jumped on me. "Coach loses huge lead . . ." and that kind of thing. Our starters were miffed, our reserves were embarrassed. Even our Principal came to me and said, in so many words, "What the heck are you doing?" That kind of thing. I mean, it was ugly. I didn't even think that many people knew we had a team. Whew. I felt like Gene Hackman in *Hoosiers* when his Principal says to him, "I'm tryin' hard to believe that you know what you're doing."

Well, obviously, I was trying to get some playing time in a varsity game for guys who didn't have enough innings under their belts, guys who were going to be starters in future years. But I learned that day what my Dad's buddy was saying, which in baseball parlance is this: "No lead is safe. You win the game you are playing, and do whatever you have to do, and worry about playing time and everybody's feelings and all the rest of it later." It was a lesson I never forgot. Shoot, I'm embarrassed retelling the story now.

Okay, but that's not the end of it. We recover from that loss, and slowly but surely we rekindle our hot streak and by the end of the year, we're leading the league. I mean we're really playing well. And my gaff is mostly forgiven. *But I haven't forgotten it.*

So right before our district tournament, we're playing at home against a team from out-of-state. And we're hitting shots and making plays and just running them off the field. And it's lopsided early, something like 13-0 in the second inning. And all the parents of our reserves are grumbling behind the backstop, "Let my kid play. The game's in hand, why doesn't he let my kid play now?" Even the starters' parents and the Principal are in the act. I can hear 'em yelling, "Come on, Coach, substitute. Let some other kids play!"

But I didn't. I kept our starters in for five innings and we 10-run ruled 'em something like 16-0. Nobody got to play but our regulars. And of course, after the game, one of our parents approached me, the parent of a backup who had not seen the field that day, but whose son had committed three errors in our botched cross-town loss earlier that year, and he says, "Why didn't you let the other kids play, Coach?'

Well, there you go. Like the Burger King motto, you can have it your way, but you can't have it both ways. You see, I was going to get criticized whether I subbed or not. The bottom line, I guess, is that there is a lot less grumbling when you win the game, and worry about everybody's else's feelings later.

Now, in the game when I didn't sub, could I have let a few kids pinch hit, or gotten some kids into the game in the fourth inning when it was 16-0? Yeah, I probably could have. And I certainly thought about it.

But maybe I was also, by keeping our regulars in the game, telling our Principal and our fans and our parents, "Look, there's only one Chief on the reservation, and it's got to be me. From now on, we play to win, no matter what. And if your son doesn't get to play, so be it. But you can't have it both ways, because we tried it the other way, it didn't work, and you barbequed me." So maybe I was thinking about that when I didn't sub at all in that lopsided, late-season blowout. Coaches are human. They have feelings. They don't enjoy being blistered in print or in person.

But it's hard, you know. It's not like football, where the coach is down on the sidelines away from the fans and can't really hear the grumbling. In baseball, the fans and parents are right there close to the action. You can hear 'em. It's hard on your family. My wife stopped going to games early in my coaching career, simply because she didn't want to listen to the complaining in the stands. "I know how hard you work, and how much time and effort you put into it, and I can't stand to hear people talk badly about you," she would say.

So no matter how supportive your wife may be, and I was blessed to have a tremendously supportive wife, the day may come when she tires of hearing the talk by the parents and fans and just decides to do something else with her time. If that happens, you've lost your biggest fan, and that's sad. I mean, she's still your fan, but she's not there at the games, and for most high school coaches, that takes some of the fun out of it.

All that said, I wouldn't trade my experience coaching high school baseball for anything. Recently I hosted a cookout for two kids who were co-captains of one of our last and best teams. They were the heart and soul of a club that set a ton of school records, some of which will probably never be broken. They are both successful adults, family men in their 40s, and we laughed and reminisced and had a wonderful time.

Late in the afternoon my catcher, one of the finest young men who ever played for me, looks right at me and says, "Coach, playing for you was one of the best things that ever happened to me. I'm a better person for having known you."

Well, I laughed it off and said something funny and changed the subject, but inside I was moved to tears, like anyone would be. That's what it's all about.

Made in the USA
Lexington, KY
10 March 2015